Modern Witch Magazine

Volume One
The Fire Within

Created By   Devin Hunter
                    Rowan Pendragon

Contributors   Devin Hunter
                    Rowan Pendragon
                    Elayne Lockhart
                    David Salisbury
                    Taylor Ellwood
                    Gede Parma
                    Yeshe Rabbit
                    Tim Titus
                    Heather Killen
                    Storm Faerywolf
                    Chas Bogan

Art By   Devin Hunter
                    Soolah Hoops

Dear Reader,

When Rowan and I decided to move Modern Witch into the world of print I was completely excited at the possibilities. I started the Modern Witch Podcast almost two years ago to the date of this publication and never in my wildest dreams did I think that the modern pagan community would invite the show and my voice into their homes with such open arms and acceptance. The show, the contributors, the fans, the spiritual work, the long nights, and the traveling have been more than worth it as I find myself here with you.

Modern Witch has become a labor of love as we have searched the modern pagan world for new and exciting voices to bring them to our community. In 2011 I was blessed to have Rowan Pendragon- bloggess extraordinaire- join me on the show as co-host and I have found her to be utterly irreplaceable. With our collaborative efforts we began to build a brand that we felt truly represented the modern witch- our stories, our craft, our hunger for knowledge. We realized just as many of you reading this have that it was time to move away from the typical witchcraft 101 and deliver something deeper and from this burning desire the Modern Witch Magazine was born.

This magazine is much more than your average magazine because we know as witches the importance of exploring our craft together. Within these pages you will be given the chance to dive into the minds and practices of some of today's top pagan authors, artists, writers, and musicians- learn new forms of magic, new ways of spiritual empowerment, and ponder the thoughts and gnosis shared here. Feel free to cut out the spell pages and add them to your own collection and while you are at it check out our amazing sponsors like The Mystic Dream, Copper Cauldron Publishing, The Sacred Well, Carnivalia, and The Living Temple of Diana.

We are proud of this product and the magic shared within and hope that you find a home here with us between the pages of Modern Witch Magazine. Notice the QR codes through-out: with your smart phones or digital device you can scan each QR code and be transported to websites, audio meditations, and more. For those of you without the ability to scan QR codes all of the links will be made available on our website www.ModernWitchMag.com .

Before you lies over 100 colorful pages of spirit, magic, and mystery. If you like what you see here shoot us an e-mail and let us know! I wish you happy reading and inspiration, may the Gods, ancestors, and guides be with you on your continued journey.

Love, Light, and all that Jazz,

Devin Hunter

Design Editor Modern Witch Magazine
Head Priest- The Living Temple of Diana
Host- The Modern Witch Podcast
www.DevinHunter.net

Celebrate Samhain with the Witches of New Orleans!

Saturday October 27th, 2012
8:00pm - 1:00am

For more information, please visit
www.neworleanswitchesball.com

Modern Witch Magazine

For Ordering info please visit our website www.ModernWitchMag.com or e-mail us at orders@modernwitchmag.com

For Ads and specs please visit our website www.ModernWitchMag.com or e-mail us at Ads@modernwitchmag.com

For general inquireies and info please visit our website at www.ModernWitchMag.com or e-mail us at info@ModernWitchMag.com

Modern Witch Magazine
(c) 2012 Modern Witch Productions

USA/San Francisco CA

ISBN:978-0615599922

Category: Metaphysical studies, new age, Magick Occult

Content Editor:
Rowan Pendragon

Design Editor:
Devin Hunter

Advertising and Marketing:
Devin Hunter
Rowan Pendragon

THE FIRE WITHIN | Spring 2012

Contact us:

ATTN: Modern Witch Magazine
1437 North Broadway,
Walnut Creek CA
94596

Info@modernwitchmag.com

Under no circumstances can any work within this print publication or digital publication be altered, reproduced, transmitted, or sent without the express written consent from the publisher. Failure to comply with copyright laws is punishable in a court of law.

Table of Contents

Modern Witch Magazine: The Fire Within   Imbolc Release 2012

8 Brighid: A Personal Relationship
   -Elayne Lockhart

Flame Wars and Tender Hearts **11**
   -Yeshe Rabbit

14 Circle Casting Part 1
   -Rowan Pendragon

Following the River **18**
   -Gede Parma

20 10 Things you can do NOW to make your magick more effective
   -Devin Hunter

Magickal Activism **26**
   - David Salisbury

33 Spell Page- Invokation of the witchcraft Goddess.

The Witch's Tree **36**
   -Storm Faerywolf

42 Pagans and the Internet
   -Rowan Pendragon

Anger: The Untamed Inner Flame **46**
   -Tim Titus

50 Interview with a Fire Spinner-Devin Hunter

Modern Witch Music: Best of Sequoia Records 54
-Devin Hunter

56 The Witch's Tree Cont.
-Storm Faerywolf

The Inner Mounting Flame 60
-Taylor Ellwood

62 Sitting your altar
- Heather Killen

Within the Cards Chapter Sampler 66
-Rowan Pendragon

74 Healing through Shamanic Fire
-Rowan Pendragon

Being the now not the then 78
-Devin Hunter

81 Spell Page: A Rite of Self Awareness from Being the Now not the Then.

Spell Page: Elemental Incense 83

86 The Magick of Wonder Woman
-Storm Faerywolf

Burning Windows: Ceromancy 92
-Chas Bogan

96 Contributor Bios

Brighid
A Personal Relationship
By Elayne Lockhart

Brighid is one of the most beloved goddesses in the Celtic pantheon. Search out her name on the Internet and over a thousand websites will come up where you can discover her attributes of healing, creativity, smithcraft, and inspiration. Her symbols include the hearth, cauldron, forge, Brighid's cross, Brighid's knot, corn dolls and Bride's bed. She is connected to animals such as cows, wrens, cats, foxes and bees. Through these websites you can learn about her mythology, family lineage, Holy day, places of worship, and that she is the patron of Bards and favors them with the gift of bells to tie on their staffs. You will also learn how she became a saint in the Catholic Church.

Brighid has been in my life for many years. She is one of the core Celtic deities I have established a rapport with. While having this working relationship with her, she has shared many things with me, such as how she likes a bowl (well) of water on the altar and that she favors yellow over the color red. A statue of her sits on my desk with a yellow candle lit before it. I can feel her standing behind me, over my shoulder, giving me guidance as I write.

Brighid has been in my life for many years. She is one of the core Celtic deities I have established a rapport with. While having this working relationship with her, she has shared many things with me, such as how she likes a bowl (well) of water on the altar and that she favors yellow over the color red. A statue of her sits on my desk with a yellow candle lit before it. I can feel her standing behind me, over my shoulder, giving me guidance as I write.

For Brighid's Fire, Imbolc, my ritual probably resembles most Pagan rituals for Brghid with maybe a few exceptions. As part of my ritual, I write a poem or create a piece of jewelry. I have a corn doll on the altar that a Druidess friend made. There is a custom of placing something on the altar for seven consecutive years at Imbolc for Brighid to bless and imbue with her energy to use during ritual. A stone I painted with a flame now holds this energy. I leave a bowl of cream and oats on the porch for Brighid's cow. I also tie green and blue ribbons on the front doorknob of our home. There are several knots tied into each ribbon and I ask Brighid to bless these with healing when she visits. The green ribbon is for physical healing while the blue one is for emotional healing. I can use these ribbons throughout the coming year for any healing work I have to do by untying one of the knots.

One of her most well known attributes is that of healing. In 1999, at our winter solstice ritual, my husband suffered one of his seizers, which triggered a heart attack. One of the people attending was a registered nurse and started CPR immediately. The paramedics came and he was taken to emergency. He was then put on life support.

Brighid, Arianrhod and Cerredwen, took up physical residence in the three CCU nurses. Brighid was a full bodied woman, a few inches taller than me, with dark hair pulled loosely up on the top of her head. Her smile radiated warmth and comfort, They were a great source of comfort and strength. My children and my (spiritual) sister were at my side as well.

On that first day when my sister and I were sitting with my husband, we both witnessed the same vision. The wall behind his bed seemed to dissolve away and there he was walking in a field of wheat with his Guru Babaji, He seemed to be asking all the spiritual questions he'd been seeking to know the answers to in this life and he looked happier than I had ever seen him.

On the second day, the doctor came into the room and informed me and my sister that my husband was brain dead. What were my wishes? My first thought was, are you kidding? But then, I knew his spirit wasn't in his body any longer, that it was just an empty shell. I could be selfish, keep his body alive and hope his spirit would return, but no. Oh, gods, give me the strength to follow my husband's wishes, to let him go. I told the doctor, who was a very sympathetic man, that my husband's wishes were never to be on life support. I asked that the machines be turned off one by one and to let his body do what it will.

As soon as the doctor left, Brighid came into the room. I chokingly told her what I had told the doctor. She hugged me and my sister to her ample bosom. Her energy was soothing and gave me strength. Later that night I received a call that my husband had passed quietly and again I could feel Brighid's arms around me.

Healing comes as time passes. I am remarried now to a wonderful man. He is truly a gift from my gods and my late husband who always wanted to see me happy. Brighid continues to be a source of creativity, inspiration and healing in my life. May she be one in your life as well.

Flame Wars
& Tender Hearts
By Yeshe Rabbit

What happens when air meets fire? The fire explodes in a riot of heat and color. What happens when the Internet hits our "hotter" emotions? We explode in colorful language and sizzling opinions.

I'm a passionate person, to be sure. Ask anyone who knows me, or read my blog: I'm chock-full of strong opinions. And I think my opinions are pretty well-formed. I read, I research, I ask around, I inform myself, I think slowly and for a long time about things…it would be easy for me to consider myself "right" as a result of these practices.

"Right" turns to "righteous" pretty quickly, doesn't it?

When a sense of "right" turns to "righteousness," it builds up heat. Righteousness is built upon a resistance to "wrong." Opposition causes friction. Friction builds heat. Heat leads to fire. It's simple science.

That heat can smolder within for days, weeks, months, years. Sometimes we have no idea we had such a strong opinion about something until we get into it with someone on the Internet, is this not true?

We're all pretty self-aware people. We know our issues, right? Except when we don't. Then, one day, you find yourself in a scalding debate in the comments section of a friend's Facebook page, and you wonder, "Who am I? I thought I was past this kind of thing. This is not who I am. But at the same time, I'm SO UPSET!"

The Internet is a very paradoxical place. It is such a warm hearth around which so many people can gather, grow, laugh and learn. It is a sterile, cold place, where emotions are unreadable and context is confusing. It is also a steamy place where sex sells and anything goes. Really, anything. The Internet is the wind, invisibly blowing over oceans and deserts and forests and mountains and snows and tropics and places we couldn't even imagine before we had it. And, like the wind, it can stoke or extinguish the flame. Sometimes it stokes the flames of anger so high that we forget that we are "real" anymore, and we become the debate instead of staying grounded in who we are as people, or the awareness that everyone else is a person, too.

There is no substitute for "meatspace," "realtime," or "facetime-in-person." There just isn't. Being people in person stokes a particular flame of community that is visceral, raw, sometimes smelly, and immediate. The phenomenal world is actually moving at a way faster pace than my Twitter feed. Yet I find myself speaking and acting far more rashly online than I do in person. In person I am mindful. I set the candle on a metal plate on the other side of the room from the billowing curtain. Online I am occasionally reactive. I know the feeling when I am doing it. The unattended flame leaps toward the curtain.

The whole cottage is threatened by my carelessness.

Why do we assume there is no one on the other end of our righteousness, our anger? Is it because they are not in the flesh in front of us? I am ashamed to admit that I have written things in emails that I would never have said in person, because I was so carried away by the heat of the moment. I feel like I am much better at balancing that now, but I still know that the seductive influence of anger is always right there behind my choice to be calm. The flame is damned attractive after all.

There have also been many times when I wrote exactly what I would have said, and it sounded kind to my ears but was widely misunderstood because the context was unclear. The flame begins to spiral in the glass, and light can be refracted so easily.

I think it's important to note that the Internet requires its own whole language. And this language is rapidly developing. Wider awareness and skillfulness with this language helps. Emoticons help. I have frequently joked that I'd like to fling a handful of happy faces into my e-mails to help people understand that I am just speaking plainly, not actually angry. Why might folks assume I'm angry? I'm definitely direct. I definitely have strong opinions. But could it be that, in addition to the justifiable portion of "Rabbit has a big personality and powerful opinions," there is also cultural conditioning in online communications to assume flaming is present if someone isn't constantly apologizing for having an opinion or being cutesy?

However it happened, we have all taken our hits online. I know I sure have. It can leave one gun shy. That little bit of extra caution after a slap is actually a good thing. It slows us down and we begin to think a bit farther down the line to a deeper, wider vision than our immediate reaction would have offered. (An aside: this is why I am so happy about Rowan Pendragon's Pagan Blog Project. It's still early in the project, but so far there is such a great atmosphere of politeness, support, and kindness. I think we owe a lot of that to Rowan's energy as the source of the fountain, but I also see that people in the project

really WANT it to go well, to create a mutually supportive clearinghouse, and to have fun doing it.)

The flame flickers and dances, the moth circles. There are two extremes: the aliveness of the flight and the sudden hot snap of death. Online communications can be like this, too. It is our responsibility to learn how to manage this emergent and life-altering resource responsibly, in a balanced way.

Part of coming to balance and steadying my own online language involves "deep freeze" periods. I have learned that every time I react from emotion, I end up being clumsy, inept, and inadvertently offensive in my tone, whether my opinion was well-formed or not. When I slow down, wait, ask myself if it is really important to get into the conversation, wait some more, form a response, wait, re-read, edit, wait, re-read, edit, wait, and then ask myself one more time if it is really important before I commit, I am much happier with the results (or non-results, when letting go is the right thing to do.)

When I put myself on deep freeze, and I don't answer an e-mail for a few days, or respond to a post, or let myself engage in the debate, I find that my tender heart reveals itself. I start wondering more about the lives of my "opponents," if they are sitting down to dinner right now, if they are unhappy in a cubicle at a dead-end job. I start to recognize my own reasons for having an unexplored pocket of negative emotion somewhere in my psyche that this communication triggered.

I start questioning my initial reaction, perhaps re-reading for clarity and finding there was a nuance that I had originally missed. Because now I am reading from a thoughtful and curious place rather than a emotional and reactive place.

The wind can gust or it can feed the flame. A careful and intelligence-based approach to online communications keeps the flame in a state of inspiration rather than destruction. This inspiring flame can then warm many in its more sustainable approach to Internet conversation.

Join me at the warm hearth of gentleness, thoughtfulness, personal responsibility, and tender hearts, won't you? There's plenty of room, and it's just toasty enough for all of us.

Circle Casting

Part 1

by Rowan Pendragon

Working with the ritual of circle casting is one of the first rituals that most Witches and Pagans learn in their formative years. If you are working with a teacher or coven you will likely have learned various ways to cast a circle and have spent hours working to perfect your skill and ability with the process. However, if you're a solitary practitioner who has learned from books, you most likely have learned the basics of circle casting and have come to a point of doing this ritual by rote but not with a real deep understanding of what you're doing and why you're doing it. If that sounds like you, don't feel bad; most solitary Witches run into this problem with at least some aspect of their practice at some time. But circle casting shouldn't be one of those. While often glossed over quickly in beginner's books, circle casting is a truly important part of ritual work.

Over the course of this year's Modern Witch Magazine, I'll be talking about circle casting a bit more in depth than you might find in a lot of books, and I'll exploring the process of circle casting in it's various parts. I'll be talking about working with your tools, evocation and invocation of the Gods, working with the elements, elemental beings, and the Watchtowers, and knowing when you really need to cast a circle or when you may be more advised to work with a simple process like that of sanctifying your space to create a sacred work space.

For this first segment we'll be taking a look at the concept overall. What is the circle? Why do we work with a cast circle? And when should you work with a circle and when can you go without one?

In Wicca and other Pagan traditions, the circle is one of the first steps to many kinds of rituals. The circle creates a space that is often said to be "between the worlds", it is in a time that has no time and a place that has no place. The circle represents your own microcosm within the Universe. You can look at it as though the Universe has pointed a spotlight in your direction when you cast this circle and created this sacred space. Both positive and negative spirits and energies see this spotlight turned on and pointed in your direction and they want to come and take a look.

In a way "circle" is a bit of a misnomer. While we cast the circle in a circular fashion, when we create the space itself energetically we're creating a sphere or a bubble. That sphere not only goes above us but below us well. We access the energies of above and blow, the energies of the land and the sky. When we stand grounded and centered within our circle we are the axis mundi, the World Tree, and the circle is the world we are supporting.

The circle performs three key functions. The one that most people tend to think of first is the function of protection. The use of circles as a form of protection has been used for centuries. Raymond Buckland gives a few examples in his book "Buckland's Complete Book of Witchcraft" that look at the use of circles outside of specific magickal work. Roman ambassadors would draw a circle around themselves with their staffs in the sand in order to show they shouldn't be attacked when in a foreign country. During the Middle Ages it's suggested that German Jews would draw a circle around the bed of a woman in labor in order to protect her from negative spirits during labor and delivery that could attack her in her weakened state. Ceremonial magicians create a circle as a form of protection for themselves while simultaneously having a triangle outside of the circle to contain entities that they call on during ritual. The use of a circle for protection is one that goes back through many, many years and today this is still one of the main functions that we look to the cast circle for.

Another important function of the circle is to contain the energy that is raised during ritual. It only makes sense that if we use the circle to help keep certain things out it's also going to keep other things in. The energy that we raise during ritual through things like chanting, dancing, drumming, and singing gathers within the space, allowing us to gather it and then release it with intention and direction.

This is often done through a process called creating a Cone of Power. By having the containing aspect of the circle there this is a much easier process than if the energy were able to disperse on its own.

The final function is sometimes more of a practical one; the circle is marked out on the floor or ground in order to physically mark where the ritual barrier is. This is often done with a piece of rope or cord. You can also use chalk for drawing the space on the ground, herbs or sachet powders can be sprinkled to mark the circle, or if the space is a permanent ritual space and the same size circle is typically used, you can paint the circle out on the floor.

The size of your circle can vary. Traditionally the coven circle is 9 feet in diameter while the solitary circle is 5 feet in diameter. These are naturally just guidelines. One of the things that anyone who's ever been in a circle will tell you is that it does create a shift in consciousness and it helps to bring us into a magickal mindset. Because of this, it's important for each individual Witch to find the circle casting method and circle size that works for them.

The circle is an energetic barrier. This energy barrier is a delicate thing. While we know that our magick may be strong, our intention and vision when casting the circle was clear, the very nature of the circle is fragile. You will hear about how you need to be careful to not "break the circle" by walking through the barrier. There is a process that can be used called "opening a door" within the circle in order to allow people to come and go from inside the ritual space if absolutely
necessary. This opening and closing weakens the circle so it should be something that is done only when truly necessary.

Within the circle we place our altar. The altar is another reflection of the magickal world and the tools are connected to the various elements as well as the God and Goddess. The altar is the focal point of all the ritual work and serves as a place for inspiration, focus, and can provide an anchor for doing astral travel work. The altar is designed to fit the specific work or celebration taking place because it works as a mirror through the worlds when inside the circle.

The tools on the altar are often seen as just that, tools. These tools are things that we have chosen to place here on the altar to help us as we need them in our circle work. Truly these are spiritual weapons; they help us to work through blockages, cutting through heavy or negative energy and directing positive energy where we need it. When we cast the circle we are working with a weapon of art. It can cut away what we don't need as well as direct the energy we do need need in the direction where we need it to be.

The use of a cast circle is not always necessary. There are times when you may not have any real energy raising happening or where you aren't planning on invite in Gods or spirits so you may not feel you need to take this step in your work. This is perfectly acceptable, however you will find that there are those practitioners, as well as authors, who will insist that you

should never do anything, even meditation, outside of a circle. Some of the reasons for this belief include the idea that you should always work with a level of protection because you don't know what you might be attracted to you through your work. Others believe that you must use this process to make the space you are working in sacred.

These ways of thinking create several problems. First is the idea that we need to always work with a high level of protection. Because of the way that circle casting is presented in many beginners books, some people have this idea that the circle is there just to protect you from things that might do you harm. In turn this breeds the idea that there are always things "out to get you" when you're working magick. While it is true that there can be a risk of attracting negative energies and entities through your work, this shouldn't be something that creates a feeling of fear or worry. If you go into your magickal work with a mindset that you are going to attract problems, you will certainly have some problems along the way.

The other concern that comes us is the idea that you need to always go through a ritualized process to make your space sacred. In some Neo-Pagan traditions the process of casting a circle is not even part of any working because the concept of all earth as sacred is held. Other traditions, including many Wiccan traditions, hold the idea that while the earth is sacred, as in the natural world outdoors, places indoors need to be made sacred because they aren't naturally sacred. If you're someone that works in the same place indoors all the time, at a set altar for example, you know that over time this becomes a very sacred space. It collects energy and becomes a special, sacred, holy place within the Universe.

When you work with the idea that you always need to have a circle to work any kind of magick it makes the idea of working magick "on the fly" a little difficult. Casting a circle in the middle of the airport in order to do some last minute safe travel magick is obviously not practical. Knowing when to work with a circle and when you don't need one is an important part of understanding the true purpose of the cast circle. This is something that we'll talk more about in a later part of this series.

In summary, think of the magick circle like this. The circle is a place that is not a place in a time that is not a time. It is both a physical place as well as a place in the other realms. It is also a process that creates sacred space and makes an area fit for magickal work and work with the Gods. When you cast a circle you are creating a boundary, both physical and energetic, which marks out the edge of your working ritual space. You are also creating a barrier, which will help in keeping out anything you don't invite while containing the energy that you have raised. All of these things are important and have their place in ritual but it is important to know why you're casting a circle when you cast one.

Next time we're going to look at crucial parts of circle casting, specifically w orking with the elements, elementals, and Watchtowers; why do we call on them and what are their true functions? How do the Watchtowers vary from just calling the elements? We'll be talking about various was to call in the elements including through visualization and through gesture, as well as the importance of choosing your words when you use your evocations to the elemental spirits.

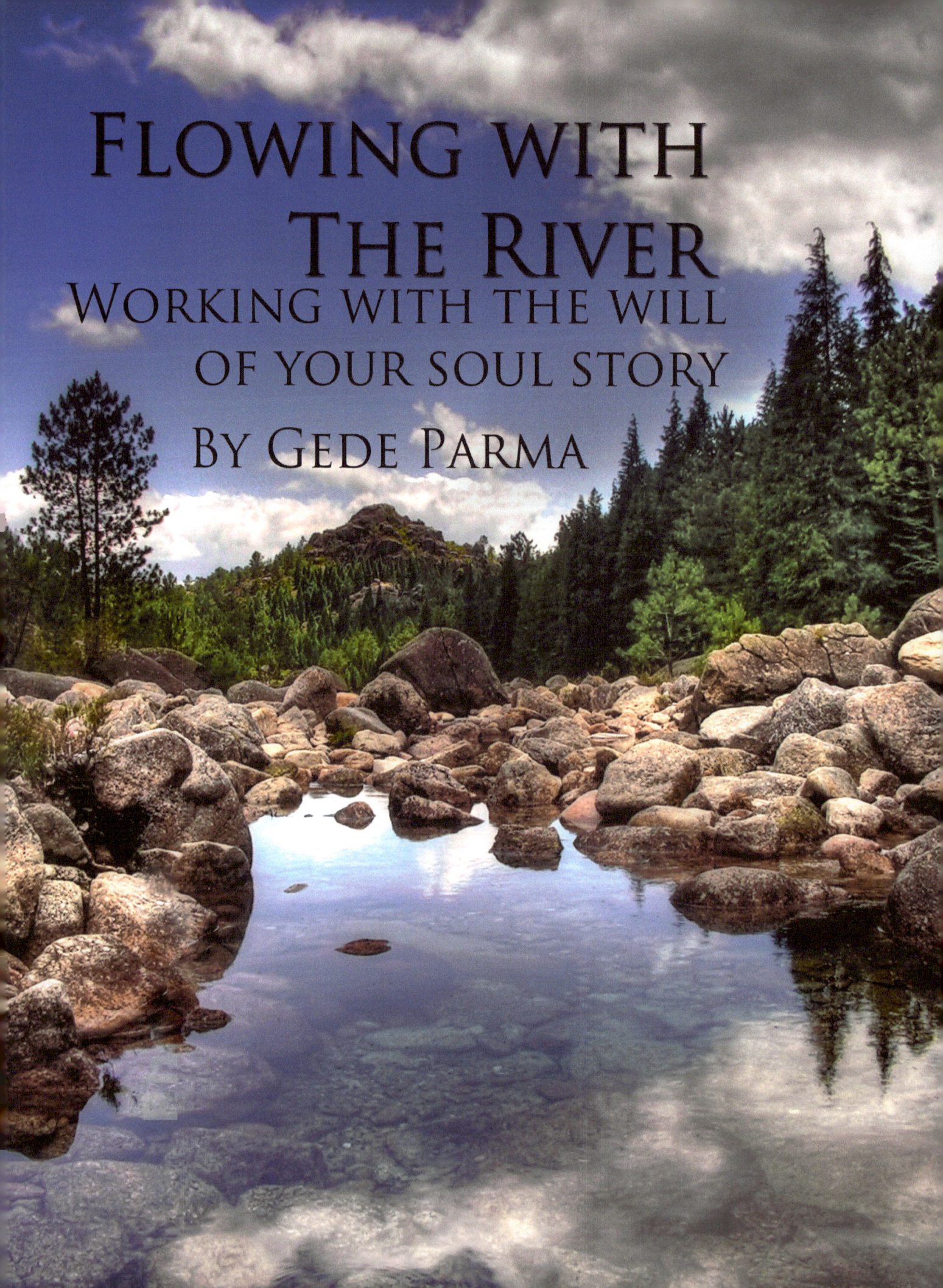

Many Witches in the modern day are not concerned with philosophy, ontology or cosmology. I am! I am devoted to these 'lofty' pursuits because I am an Ecstatic Witch – a Mystic Witch – perpetually seeking more and more of my Own Holy Self and longing to dance with the Infinity of Being as a consciously-affirmed potency.

Philosophy, meaning love of wisdom, is important to Witchcraft because it facilitates an opening of the soul to the innate wisdom which surrounds and infuses us at all times. By sitting with each other and speaking our souls and sharing our stories we enter the flow of the Divine Will – of the Living Limitless Cosmos. But what of the potency which expresses us as distinct, autonomous and vital in and of ourselves? This is the Mystery – that we are separate for Love's sake – to engender deeper intimacy within the Body and Being of God of which we intrinsically a part. To be whole with God Herself we first must come to wholeness with all the pieces of Self. When Self meets All-Self the Holy Centre is opened within us and the Infinite concentrates inside of us as we become the Living Power of the Unfolding, Desirous Being of All Things.

When our souls have stories we enter into Myth, when we become Myth we walk with the Gods, and when we walk with the Gods we become Gods. We are in our power – our divine birth-right to know fully our divine seed-origin.

The soul-story is not a pre-ordained proscription of events to befall each of us as we deepen, neither is it a story we tell ourselves; it is a story which writes itself as we dance with the Divine. It becomes a living landscape that we journey through. It is the River of Will which provides the current and momentum to the shifting of the soul within the landscape.

The River of Will is the spirit to the substance of who we are; it is the fire (ironically) of the heartland and it shines as a beacon – it sings to us to draw near and enter the Life stream. Do we choose to sit on the banks of our Rivers and watch the current flow, idly or casually dipping our toes in, or do we breathe in, dive in, surrender and let the flow guides us? We might even swim speedily along with the support of the current, but this is not a dynamic which the River can support for long. If this was kept up by a limited and only ego-driven intent we might miss details in the landscape or ultimately exhaust our capacities and sink to drown. It is wise to step into the momentum of the River of Will, attune with it and surrender in trust to its divine flow. Thus do we in truth realise the vastness and particularities of our soul-story and move with grace and authenticity.

What is the way of the Goddess? What is the Infinite Creativity but Her River of Will? When we are in the flow of our Rivers we flow in the Great Work of Mystery and make magick with the Blessed Beauty of the Shining Soul.

When we are in wholeness ourselves and cultivating Sovereignty of Self by being present in Own Holy Self we become self-possessed and free. For the freedom of the Shining Soul is Splendour, because in freedom we recognise Beauty – the Crown of All Sovereignty. We enter the Covenant of the Crown; we all share in the same authority. We are guided by the deepest and oldest Potency of All – the Seat of the Great Eye. She who opens to behold and witnesses wonder and rejoices in it.

Will the I become the Eye?

Alright so we are all guilty of having a spell or two go wrong in our day. There is nothing worse than having a spell mishap or to have a spell you really need to work flub. If you are sick of not feeling your magick, not seeing the results, and not being as successful in spell casting and ritual work as you would like here are ten things you can do right now to make your magick better, faster, and stronger!

1) Present tense makes it happen NOW.

If there is one thing we have learned from the new-age movement it is the power of the mantra. Mantras are never spoken in a past or future tense, nor do they include negatives such as the words "not, won't, lack, etc." When you are casting a spell or performing a ritual and you need the energy to manifest be sure to think very clearly about how you are projecting your magick. To stand in circle and say, " I don't want _____ to happen, but want _____ instead!" is very different from " I am _____ ." Ideally our spells and rituals that involve the need for money, love, healing, etc. should be done in the present tense. For example: " I have all the money I need, it flows to me and from me, through me." or " Johnny is cured, his cuts and bruises are healed."

It makes all the difference in the world to allow our magick to begin the instant we cast rather than an easy to forget about slow moving current. Be in the now and your magick will too.

2) Don't Yo-Yo your magick!

One of the biggest mistakes we make as witches is the yo-yoing of our magick. When we cast a spell or perform a ritual we must let it do it's job. In some cases spells or rituals will require an extended period of time to cast however once it is done we must let it do it's job. When we yo-yo our magick we are sending it out there and then not letting it go, often because we are anxious, stressed, worried, etc. By obsessing over it working or not working you are bringing it right back to you because it was never a completed thought process and that means your were not clear in intention or will. It is our job as the witch to not hold onto the magick we create but to treat it as a bird that has to fly. If we cage the magick than we are trapping our own will and crossing ourselves. Set it into motion then refocus on the signs around you, how the universe is communicating with you, etc.

Often we are too busy looking for the end result that we don't see the process unfolding. Chances are, the universe is letting you know what to do next or is sending you a sign that the magick is on it's way.

3) Connect to something bigger.

Connecting to guides, Gods, angels, allies, and ancestors gives you the ability to tap into an infinite source of power- power that has personality. The more we work with our allies in a spiritual and shamanic way the better we establish our own psychic senses and the better we can receive messages, channel power, and make adjustments when needed.

I know you have heard us say this before but- you absolutely must honor your allies as you would honor your physical ones. These spirits and archetypes come with personality and personality makes them unique. Simply asking for an ally that you have never met to aide you in magick won't cut it. Would you give five dollars to a random person on the street? Chances are you will walk right past them! However if your friend asked you for five dollars you would almost always help them. It is actually kind of rude to ask for a favor then get upset when the person says no. Get to know your allies and they will get to know you.

4) Show Respect!

Most witches invoke everything from guardians to primordial Gods into their work and then cut the devocation corner by reciting a half-hearted memorized dialogue with no soul. We have to stop and think; magick is like sex, build-up is important and foreplay is essential to a healthy exchange of life-force, if however we get to the good stuff and then don't stick around to let our partner finish- well then you are kind of an ass.

Be respectful and understand the intimacy of the work you are doing, the exchange of power from you to your allies and from your allies to you. Half-hearted devocations are the equivalent to hanging-up on someone mid-sentence. By spending as much time and energy releasing your allies as you do invoking them you are allowing a relationship of respect to build and in the long term that is essential. Think of it like this- when you are dead and in the ground and someone invokes your spirit from beyond the grave, you are going to want to be treated well and with respect, and if not what kind of havoc would you reek in their lives?

5) Know the momentum.

When casting spells we should be aware of the vessel and momentum we are working with. If the spell requires you to spend seven days making affirmations than spend as much time each day connecting to the energy. If the momentum of a spell requires a slow-steady crawl like a 'honey jar spell' to sweeten someone up, be sure not to forget about it. If you make wards for your home, car, or office, be sure to feed them! Often we create spells and invite spirits into our home then let their candles, bottles, bags, etc. get dusty! In order for your spells to be alive you have to treat them like they are. If your spell is a one-shot spell be sure to pack a powerful punch in the beginning then let it go! Feeding spells that are not meant for multiple castings will do the exact opposite of what you want them to do. By this I mean if you cast a spell to get rid of a block on your path, don't keep revisiting the spell, be strong and centered in the now and trust in your work, by revisiting it over and over again you may just be found guilty of number two!

Knowing the vessel of your magick is just as important and goes hand and hand with momentum. Some spells might use longer burning candles, require extended periods of time in a specific environment, continual feeding, require building over several days, and some spells may require objects being charged in one environment and then to be moved to another for. Before you twitch your nose be sure to outline how, when, for how long, etc. Getting the details straight ahead of time will help make magickal life much easier.

6) Remnants are still active.

One thing that always gets my goat is when I see someone burn a candle then throw away the remnants. The last time I saw someone do that it was the left-overs of a money spell they cast and guess what happened? If there is one thing hoodoo taught us it's that the proper care of our spell remnants is crucial for their success.

Be sure not to throw the baby out with the bath-water- unless you are sure that IS the point to begin with. I am reminded of a spell that required me to bury the remnants in a grave-yard, I of course forgot this part and after the remnants sat their for a few days I finally threw-out the left overs and went about my business. Within three days everything that I worked so hard for regarding this spell went in the gutter.

Your spell remnants are much more than the skin off the chicken you didn't want to eat or the peas that got too close to your mashed potatoes, you can't just throw them away like they are the unwanted left-overs from your mothers dry cooking. They are still vibrating and resonating with the pulse of your spell work so take the time to consider your options. Here is a pointer I learned from Dorothy Morrison and M.R. Sellars- If you want it to come to you, bury the remnants by the front door (yes a flower pot works well too!), if you want the energy to stick around bury the remnants in your backyard, if you want to remove the energy bury the remnants near running water. As always be respectful of mother earth and don't go using the river as a spiritual dumping ground. Be sure to know where you buried them and make sure no-one else will have the ability to find them!

7) Fare-weather witches make fare-weather magick.

When we do magick only when it is convenient or only go to ritual when it is convenient we are only being witches when it is convenient. This practice produces quite the issue in the long-run as it encourages the growth of blocks that keep you from being an effective spell caster. We should be plugged in as much as possible and whenever possible. Spell casting is the easy part, being able to cast a spell in an instant is the hard part. The less time we spend within the presence of the magickal current of energy the harder it is to grow as a witch. This is why many witches feel like they can't move beyond a specific skill set or that they are spiritually 'stuck.' Sit your altar, check your connectedness and if you feel like you are slacking off, chances are you are right my friend.

8) CLEAN YOUR TOOLS!

Running a spiritual supply store has taught me a thing or two. I see people come in everyday who are looking for pieces for the spell they want to cast, pick up a red candle and say 'Yeah this is what I need for that money spell' then realize the spell actually needed a green candle instead. They then pick up 5 different green candles before they make their final choice and go with the pillar candle. Someone else then comes in and picks up that same red candle person A had in their hands convinced they were going to use it, and person B decides they want to purchase it for their love spell. This goes on and on, essentially before you actually light the candle you are going to use at least five to ten other folks have touched it and put their own intention onto it.

So often we forget to prepare ourselves and our tools/ingredients to get them ripe for the magick we want to create. We see a candle, buy it, spend an hour figuring out the rest of how it is all going to work and then just sit down and do the spell. We should have all that figured out before hand and then every step of that spell should be prepared as if each step were a spell of it's own. All your ingredients are like the ingredients in a recipe, if you don't clean the spinach your salad will have sand in it, not to mention the recent outbreaks of e-coli. That's the thing, others people's energy can quickly become the germs and bacteria that causes your magick to get sick, not work properly, or not work at all.

Salt, Salt, Salt. Mixing salt in water then using the water to cleanse your tools normally does the trick as salt is known for it's ability to disperse etheric patterns. Here is a tip: purchase a plastic storage container or something similar, every time you go to the grocery store buy a container of salt, table salt will work just fine, and add it to the contain

Devin Hunter

The Psychic Medium that understands YOUR spirituality

Long distance and in-person sessions starting at just

$35.00/15 min!

Tarot/Sensitive Sessions

Long Distance Healing Sessions

Spirit Guide Communication

Spirit Contact

Magick and Conjure work

"Devin is THE BEST psychic consultant I have ever been to, he is spot on every-time and I love watching everything he says come to fruition." -Nimaat G

"My life has been changed forever after my sesion with Devin. What a gift from the Goddess!" Kathy K

"I have a hard time relating to most psychics, they look at me weird when I tell them I'm a witch. Not only is Devin a witch, but he gave me the advice I needed to fix the issues. He is the real deal!" - Tony B

Every Session is personal, empowering, and real. no thrills, no hidden fees, just you, me, and Goddess.

www.DevinHunter.Net
(562) 99-WITCH

er until it is about half way full. Purchase a small piece of citrine and place it in the container as well. This container of salt and citrine is the equivalent of a magickal bathtub for your tools and supplies. When you get your magickal items place them in the container over night before using them. The citrine is a self-cleansing stone and will aide in the cleansing of your tools and supplies.

9) Be an engineer.

Engineer, pioneer, same difference when it comes to your relationship with your magick. Don't be afraid to color outside the lines from time to time and experiment with the tools at your disposal. We reference ways other people have done their magick or we cast spells that have been tested and approved like those found in books or online but most witches don't create their own spell work. Reading and pouring yourself into a book can only take you so far and at some point you have to put the book down and pick up your wand! At any level of knowledge there is opportunity to take a hands-on approach to creating your own unique magick. Let others inspire you but don't give up your own brand of witchcraft! Become an engineer to the magick, create it, change it, move it, and let your higher self guide you through the process.

10) Daily practice is irreplaceable.

One of the biggest lessons I have learned is the importance of creating a daily practice. This means that everyday I align myself, ground, center, and do cleansing work. Here is the thing; we are people who work in the energy field, whether you are an actively witch'n it up or are out about in the world you just can't "turn off" your magick. Everyday we are surrounded by other people with lord knows what type of issues, hopes of their own, maybe even magick of their own and all that rubs off on you. Before we know it we are surrounded by etheric clutter, our sense of place in the universe is off balance, and then we go to bed just to get up and collect more junk the next day. So many of our problems energetically come from simply not being as energetically cleaned and aligned as we could be. Yes, do a cleansing on yourself everyday- I'm not implying that you have poor hygiene just that if you take a shower daily you should cleanse your energy body daily as well. The less astral stuff sticking to you the better and your magick most certainly can tell!

Magickal Activism
The Passion of Fire
By David Salisbury

I am an activist. I have been for most of my life in one form or another and the work I've done with it has morphed and evolved as many times as I have.

In my work for animals I've gone on secret investigations to uncover the abuse of Asian elephants in the circus, barged into Donna Karen's office and demanded she ditch fur, laid naked and "bloodied" in the middle of Times Square to stop bullfighting, and sat in a cage for a day at Princeton University to stop animal testing. For LGBT equality I've marched in most major cities on the east coast for marriage rights or the repeal of Don't Ask, Don't Tell and took a full time job at the largest LGBT rights organization in the country. Though the campaigns have been as varied as my many interests, they all share a common link, a point of origin that is subtle to most, the fire of passion that burns in every heart.

Both passion and activism in general are words that carry heavy baggage for some people. Activism might conjure images of loud protesters climbing street poles and screaming on megaphones. Passion might make you think of someone being overly-interested in something, to the point of obsession. The English language is complex and this complexity can create confusion surrounding the types of activities activists engage in and the inner fires that fuel them. The key to better understanding activists is to learn about what drives them.

Passion's Fiery Root

This is a magazine for Witches so let's get a little mystical here. In the system of chakras that most magickal people are familiar with, fire is linked to the root chakra, the red orb of energy located near the base of the spine called the muladhara. This chakra is responsible for sex and survival, among other things. In this case, our need to survive as a race or to make our planet survive is the point of origin for the activist. Most activists will tell you that they feel deeply obliged to "do something" when a terrible act is committed.

This is a type of instinct but it's much more than that. This strong desire to contribute to change is caused by an active and fiery root chakra sending signals to all other areas of the body. It is saying "Rise up! Protect! Defend it or you'll be next!" It is said to be the seat of kundalini where the coiled serpent of energy awaits until it rises upon activation. It also governs personal power and can be considered a cause of what makes activists feel empowered to act at all.

When we look at the ritual weapon associated with fire we find knives like the athame, boline, and white knife of ceremonial magick. The material of the athame is forged in the flames and takes on a shape that is constructed from the heat and pressure the fire brings. From this "boiling point", the malleable metal is formed and cut into a sharp and powerful tool. A person with a low boiling point can get "overheated" about things and so upset that they feel too overwhelmed to do anything about it. This is activist burnout and isn't all that different from the spiritual burnout experienced by some Witches who have positions of leadership within their communities. However, the Witch who is as sharp and balanced as her blade can temper this by directing all that fire where it needs to go.

The sword in general is a fine symbol to use for the activist. However peaceful, the activist really is engaging in a battle for what they think is right. Their moral compass points only in the direction of justice and they feel no other option but to fight for that justice. In Gnostic terms we can look at the flaming sword of Archangel Michael. Michael can cut us free from the restrictive entrapments that keep us from our true potential.

Don't mistake him for a friendly cherub though! Michael and his flaming sword are often summoned to cut down enemies and deliver swift justice to the oppressed.

The nature of fire is to bring immediate and dramatic change, more so than any other element. The other elements aid us in the overall process of transformation and rebirth, but it is fire that has the power to turn things to dust in nearly an instant. For this reason, we must be careful with how we use it. In the case of activism, uncontrolled fire shows up in extremism. When the inner flame is burning so strong that it cannot be tempered or directed, the result can be violence and rage against the perceived evil-doer. This of course is almost always ineffective activism. Does the activist perpetrator of violence change something when they cause harm? Yes, but that harm as an agent of the uncontrolled fire tends to rebound right back on their own campaign.

How then can a prospective activist channel the mighty power of flame, and have it not overtake them? There are many tried and true methods both magickal and mundane. If you're engaging in any sort of activist campaign on the short or long term, the following tips might help you keep up your energy, avoid burnout, and be the most effective you can be.

Meditation and daily energy work -

Being consistent with working with energy means that we can handle more of it at once.

It also means that we're more likely to know what to do if the energy gets out of control. A few months ago at the soup kitchen I volunteer at, a couple guests were starting to get violent with each other, which is quite rare for this venue. Stepping aside from my station, I began to draw the fire out from between them and replaced it with cooling blue light from the spirits of water. Practicing work like this means you won't freeze up in panic if you ever need to use it.

Rest -

Taking breaks from activism and service are extremely important. Resting helps you avoid burnout, keeps you energized, and just generally keeps you from feeling emotionally and energetically overwhelmed. After all, you're no good to your cause if you tax yourself to the point of being sick! Even if you don't take significant time off, be sure to ground and center frequently if you find yourself in a place where you're performing activism every day.

Make a Change Altar -

A Change Altar is a special area you set up specifically for the campaign(s) you're working on. For example, if I'm doing the circus work I mentioned in the beginning, I might decorate this altar with images of elephants, their habitats, and even Ganesh, the elephant god who removes all obstacles standing in the way of change. I might put my materials like leaflets or signs on the altar to be blessed and charged.

Work with activist ancestors -

Call upon great activists who are now in the ranks of the Mighty Dead to assist your work. Martin Luther King Jr., Mahatma Ghandi, and even Thomas Jefferson are all examples of spirits of the past you can honor and pray to for help. Every Samhain in DC we have an event called "Drumming at the Jefferson" where we gather at the Jefferson Memorial at drum in honor of the founding people of our country. We ask them to protect our nation and grant our leaders (and citizens) the wisdom and courage to do what is right.

Through a combination of any of the methods above, you're sure to formulate a nicely balanced system for whatever campaign you approach. If you're new to magickal activism, learning to blend in these energetic tactics with what you're already doing will lead you to discover you're own unique system.

Magickal Activism

In addition to the methods above that consider a physical and spiritual approach, we can also consider the magicks available to us for this work. Using spells and charms to create revolution is nothing new. Just ask any Witch in the Reclaiming Tradition and they'll tell you. Fixing up a spell ahead of time is a great way to prepare for a demonstration or public hearing. I'll share a few of my favorites here, but combinations of any preferred spell for justice and protection will wield results similar to the spells here.

Charm to Protect a Protester

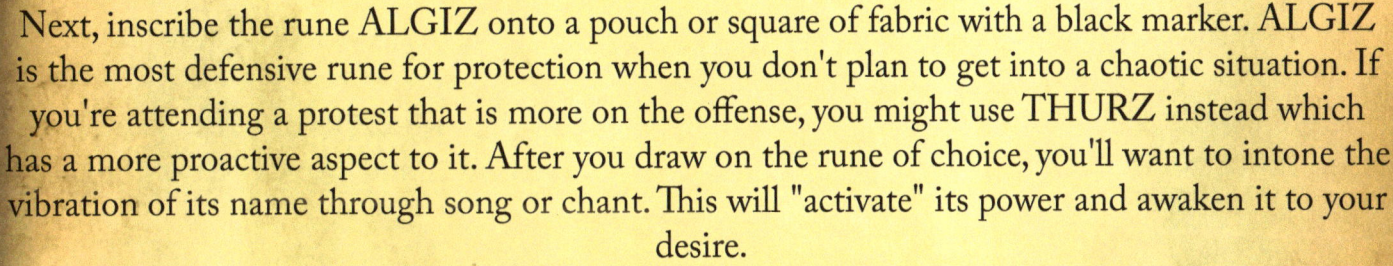

Combine three of any of these herbs and crush well:
-Marigold
-Dragon's Blood
-Rue
-Sage
-Mistletoe
-Red Sandalwood

Next, inscribe the rune ALGIZ onto a pouch or square of fabric with a black marker. ALGIZ is the most defensive rune for protection when you don't plan to get into a chaotic situation. If you're attending a protest that is more on the offense, you might use THURZ instead which has a more proactive aspect to it. After you draw on the rune of choice, you'll want to intone the vibration of its name through song or chant. This will "activate" its power and awaken it to your desire.

Now you're ready to pour the herbs into the pouch. If you have a square of fabric, you can pour the herbs in and tie the corners together. To secure the bag, tie it with red or black string. As you tie up the bag, you can use this time to infuse the charm with your overall goal, which is to stay safe and guarded during your campaigning.

Spell to Ignite the Flame of Passion

Use this spell when you feel like you're on the brink of activist burnout, or you need a reminder of why the work you're doing is important. Summoning the passion of fire can bring intense results so you should be really sure that you need this energy to aid you.

What you'll need:
Red 7-day candle
Herbs of Bay Laurel, Red Pepper, and Chili
Photo of yourself

With the photo of yourself in hand (preferably doing some sort of campaign work), begin to imagine yourself in the midst of doing your activism and loving every moment of it. Contemplate why you do what you do and the sense of purpose it gives you back in return.

With this feeling of purpose anchored well, light the candle and summon the flames of passion;

Spirit of the heart so red
of blood that pumps through every heart
Awaken to this Witch's need
and bless this sacred art.
Fires of the living flame
of passion burning fierce and strong
Arise and come to burn within
and live upon this song.

You can say the above multiple times or return to your visuals (or better yet, both!). As the wax melts and begins to generate a liquid pool, add small pinches of the mixture of herbs. Laurel and the peppers grant courage, success, and the power of fire. We toss them into the candle as an offering to the fire spirits and to align our will with multiple elements at once.

When a large pool of wax has gathered, carefully pour some out over the photo of yourself. Pour it in the general shape of a heart if you can manage it. Sprinkle the rest of the herbs over the wax on the photo. Once it dries, you can keep it on your altar as a daily way to ignite the flames of passion for whatever your cause may be.

Change Dust

This is a simple spell that can be put together with little prep and used as frequently as you like. Magickal powders have a strong background in the Hoodoo arts and you'll find uses for them for every occasion. This "change dust" is a powder to magickally affect change with the campaign you're working on. Simply blend together any three of these herbs:

Vervain
Bail
Ginger
Cinnamon
High John
Rowan
Winters Bark

After blending together, you'll want to turn them into the finest powder possible. This requires the use of a good mortar and pestle. Some prefer using a blender, but I feel that the greater connection is established with the physical grinding of the herbs through the hands. Sprinkle the dust at the site of wherever your action is. Even if you're signing online petitions, you can keep a store of it right by your keyboard.

Why Witches Care

I very firmly believe that Witchcraft is a religion of change. When something is happening that we know is not right or not serving our Work in the world, we seek to change it. The nature of the Witch is to bend and flow with the currents of life with grace and integrity. We see this in the number of Witches today who advocate for ethical lifestyles whether they relate to service to humans, the environment, or to animals. If you asked a room full of Witches if they've ever participated in a demonstration or helped field a petition, I'd wager the number would be quite high. Just look at the huge amount of Pagans who are involved with the current Occupy movement for more proof of this. This is because Witches often feel what's called an "awareness obligation."

Awareness obligation means that once you know the truth about some type of injustice, you tend to feel morally obligated to either not contribute to it, or to change it entirely. If you know your neighbor is abusing a child next door, chances are you would feel morally obligated to stand up and report it to the appropriate authorities. Because Witches are used to working with the unseen world, we tend to extend this sentiment to things that are even further outside of our experience. An aware Witch is likely to feel the same type of passion to help the child next door as he is to help a starving child in Indonesia. Working with "invisible forces" certainly gives us a leg up in our understanding of other plights.

Its more than a sense of obligation though. The Witch claims a certain innate power, complex and sometimes mysterious. The power is complex because of where it comes from. Arguably, Witches are most concerned with working with the powers of the natural world. The Earth, its environment and all the cosmos are a limitless source of energy, an avenue of connection that can be tapped into at any time. With this complexity arise questions that we must ask of ourselves. If my power is connected to the natural world (and those whole live within it), then shouldn't I be interested in nurturing and sustaining the source of that power? If I am but a stand in the great web of life, then I certainly have an interest in keeping the web whole and strong.

Being an effective magickal activist requires several key factors; insight, passion, purpose and method. All of these arise from fire. Through a strong relationship with fire and the inner flames of our passion, we discover that we truly do have the power to change the world.

WE HAVE SOME GREAT THINGS BREWING!

COPPER CAULDRON PUBLISHING

Copper Cauldron Publishing is an independent publisher of metaphysical and neo-pagan books, including the work of award-winning author Christopher Penczak (*The Temple of Witchcraft* series and others). Look for our books at your favorite pagan and New Age retailer, major online retailers, and direct from the author's website: *www.christopherpenczak.com*. Find us at our website and on Facebook to keep up on the latest Copper Cauldron news and releases!

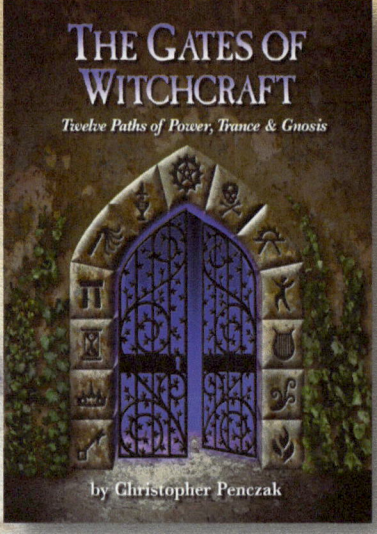
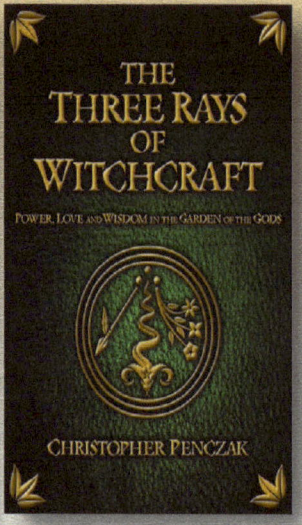

INFO@COPPERCAULDRONPUBLISHING.COM • WWW.COPPERCAULDRONPUBLISHING.COM

Come, come whoever you are, Even if you've broken your vows 10,000 times, Come, come again.

Journeyers, wanderers, lovers of life - Come, come, come!

This caravan has love to spare - Come, come, come!

Come As You Are Coven is an open, eclectic, drop-in coven providing community rituals in the San Francisco Bay area. Our mission is to create safe, loving, magickal space for all those who wish to participate in community rituals. We gather for ritual in the fashion of the ancient rural villages and tribes – all are invited and welcome as members of the community.

Our Coven is governed by three sacred tenets:
1. We honor one another's unique spiritual practices, and seek to enrich our sense of community with diversity.
2. We accept one another's divinity as inherent and non-negotiable.
3. We believe that we are each qualified to determine our own personal path, and share our experiences and thoughts in a spirit of generosity, without presumption.

Our Offerings

Sabbats For All
CAYA follows our own Wheel of the Year, honoring the seasonal cycles of birth, death, transformation, and rebirth. Our ritual year begins with Samhain and ends with Mabon. Sabbats are open to all and everyone is welcome.

CAYA Sprouts
Sabbat rituals specifically designed for children up to age ten. However, all self-identified families are welcome to attend.

The Grove of Artemis (East Bay) and The Grove of Hekate (South Bay)
The Groves are Full Moon ritual circles open to all self-identified women.

The Brotherhood of the Moon (East Bay)
A Full Moon ritual circle open to all self-identified men.

Perhaps you are a curious seeker, perhaps an experienced practitioner. If you wish to contribute your own unique, authentic, and benevolent beliefs to a community that is accepting, empowering, diplomatic, ethical and fair, then *Come As You Are and Be Welcome.*

Visit our website for complete information at www.cayacoven.org

Invokation of the Witchcraft Goddess
(Version One)

INVOKATION OF THE WITCHCRAFT GODDESS
(Version One)

The Goddess comes to us with many faces, some call her Diana, some call her the Morrigu, some call her Astarte, but all know her. She is the mother of the universe, that which is protective of her kin and loving to her children. She is strong, she is divine, and she is all. This invocation has aided me well and is done when I honor my mother, it goes back to the very beginning of my practices.

You will need
Silver candle. Circle of salt, Quartz or Amethyst

To call the Goddess do not despair, she is the mother and you her heir. Take the time to shape your round, and light the candle she is profound. Quartz and Amethyst do assist, for you'll need guidance in her midst. Sit and focus on the prize, surround yourself with light, it would be wise. Take three breaths and here you go, She is the mother, you're soon to know.

Goddess, Great mother, I your child call to you.
Mother, Life giver, I your child call you here.
Triple Goddess, I your child ask your presence.
Goddess, Wise one, I your child call to you.
Mother, Creator, I your child invite you here.
Triple Goddess, I your child ask your presence.
Goddess, Wise one, I your child call to you.
Lady, Mother, I your child invite you here.
Triple Goddess, I your child call your presence NOW!

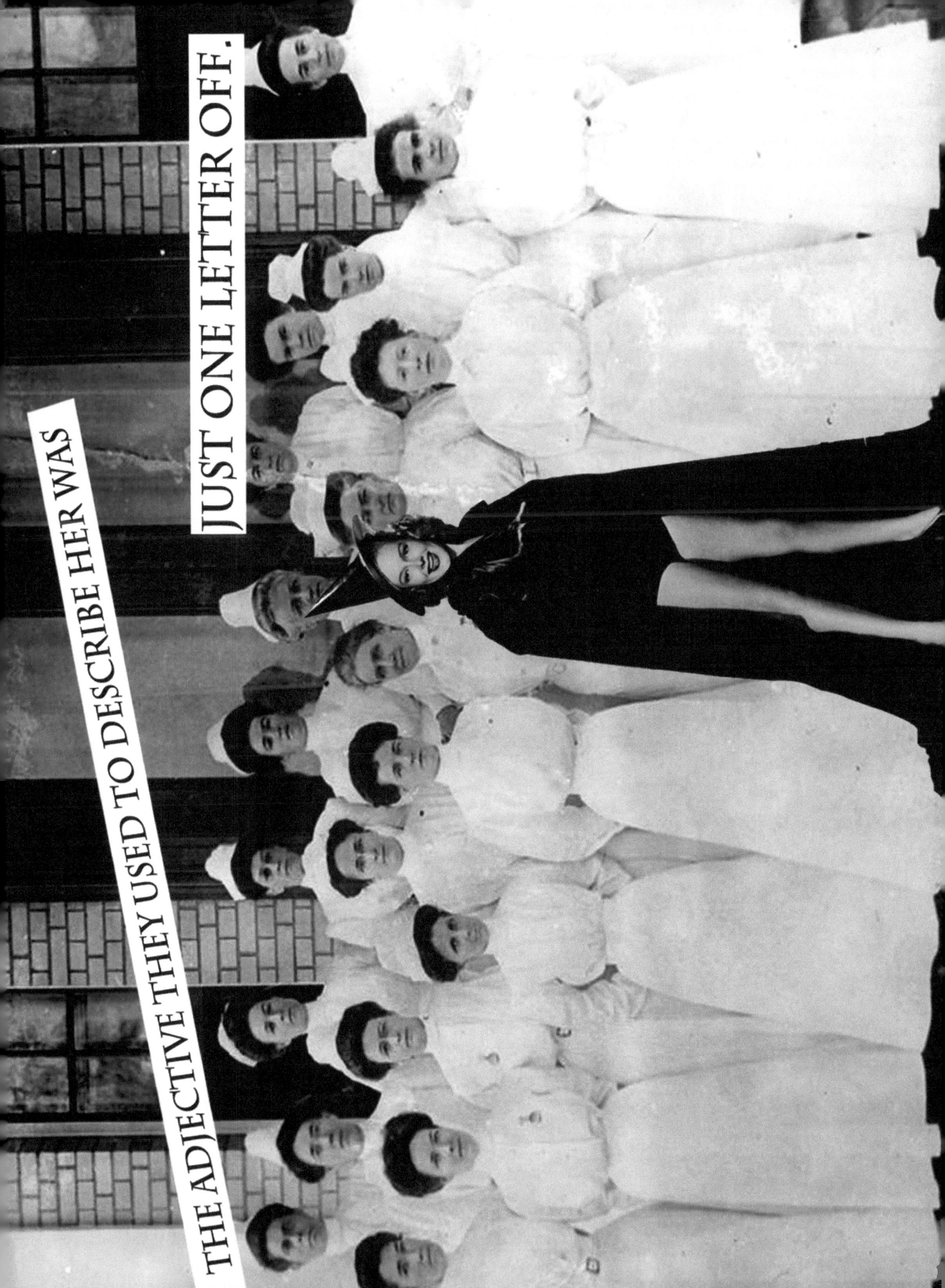

THE ADJECTIVE THEY USED TO DESCRIBE HER WAS JUST ONE LETTER OFF.

The Witch's Tree

And, lo! There grows a faery tree,
where do four roads and powers meet
And on it many roses bloom With
starlight; a myriad of hues
Into its secrets we are drawn By
midnight, sunset, noon, and dawn
And the mysteries of the deep
Well of stars where the Old Ones sleep
And dream of future things now
past. To draw together the small and vast.
And thus conjoined; two flames
in one The witches' fire has nowbeen won.

Tradition, Innovation, and my path In Between.
by Storm Faerywolf

I have been practicing some form of witchcraft since I was a child. During the years of my ongoing and deepening practice I have experienced a pretty full spectrum of working, having spent several years as a book-taught solitary, a member of a self-formed eclectic coven, an initiate of a Wiccan coven, and a traditionally trained and initiated priest in what is often called 'the traditional Craft'. My magical training has been informed by several traditions, ideas, and experiences, all of which have deepened my understanding of spirituality, as well as the quality of my magical work. I have been practicing witchcraft for a significant majority of my life and so I am confident in my vision and my approach which draws from many sources to suit my specific needs, which in my opinion, is exactly the point of witchcraft to begin with.

What I have learned is that not only are there many paths to understanding the universe and our place within it, but that it is also necessary to experience –and even embody—these different ideas, techniques, cultures, world-views, etc. While each on their own may offer some modicum of wisdom, they each also possess within them the potential for tyranny which serves to enslave the ego and hinder the spirit.

I began my witchcraft career by reading as many books on the subject as I could get my hands on. In them were described various spells and techniques for altering consciousness and performing magic alongside myths and stories that sought to describe the universe in terms that were specific to a particular culture or tradition. Having armed myself with the knowledge of a few different approaches I began to practice on my own and experiment with what I had read; sometimes with great results, others not so much.

I joined with others of like mind and we began to practice together; perhaps to try a ritual out of a book, but more often to write our own using what we had learned as a general framework. This is where the power really started flowing; each of us began to trust our own inner voice just enough to allow us to drop the ego's fear of being "wrong" and we just began to "wing it"; allowing inspiration to guide us in the moment and seeing what came of it.

It was a tremendously transformative time; the experiences that I shared with that group shaped my understanding of magic, giving me an experiential framework for magic and practices that I would later read about or be re-introduced to in other contexts. I was able to deepen my spiritual awareness in ways I had only dreamed of previously, and my confidence in my abilities grew by leaps and bounds.

Our group worked consistently until, due to that little thing called "life", we disbanded as members moved across the country to deal with family issues and pursue other interests. I took what I had learned and practiced solitary once more, but now with a renewed understanding of how it all worked and fit together.

Around this time I began to read tarot professionally; at a bookstore here, at an event there; just enough to keep me working with the public, a far more taxing experience than simply reading for your friends or those whim you otherwise are familiar with. This gave me a sense of confidence as well; people would ask me for spiritual and magical advice and I found that I had a talent for helping people develop spiritually.

After several years of working in this way I decided that what I really needed was a tradition; an established set of methods for working magic and a culture to tie it all together. And I knew just the tradition for me. After reading Starhawk's The Spiral Dance I was completely struck by her stories of Victor Anderson and the Faery(1) tradition and I was hooked. It possessed something for me that other traditions did not: a sense of belonging, a familiarity that I couldn't exactly describe. I set out to find a teacher, but this wasn't as easy as I had first hoped.

While looking, I found a coven in my area that was centered in another Craft tradition. While I had met other people and groups who practiced the Craft, they generally seemed to be formed of people who wanted to learn the Craft instead of from people who had learned it and wanted to teach others.

I often found myself in a leadership role in these groups, which didn't satisfy my need to learn more about witchcraft and magic. But this group seemed different. The members were all older than me (I being a mere 20 years old at the time –the youngest member of the coven; the others being at least 10-45 years my senior). They had a Book of Shadows that they used to perform their seasonal and passage rituals… the members all had titles that described their function in the coven, and they all seemed to be versed in the ways of magic. Or, at least it seemed that way in the beginning.

After a short while I was initiated into the 1st degree. I still remember the feeling of elation I felt when the coven circled around me to chant and raise a cone of power… revealing to me their secret name of the Goddess, and channeling the power of the cone into me at its apex. I felt opened up to a higher power; I experienced a soaring sense of bliss that to this day I can recall viscerally. I was flying high for a week afterward and felt very accomplished indeed. No longer was I simply a "student" or "enthusiast", I was an "official" witch!

The High Priest began to groom me to take over his position and so I began attending extra meetings and helping him teach public classes. I wrote materials, I assisted in rituals; anything that was asked of me I dutifully did, all in the name of studying and serving the Craft.

Then I started to notice something; while the group seemed to put on a good show for the newbies there were certain things that started to seem… "off", at least to me. Such as the need for the members to read all of their rituals directly out of their book (which left many of the rituals feeling two-dimensional and lifeless), or the lack of magic done at a meeting, opting instead for potluck dinners consumed within a magic circle. The High Priestesses would never just speak from their heart or even memorize the rituals they were to perform.

And their lackluster performances seemed in line with someone who was just learning the Craft more so than of the rank that they supposedly earned. Another was that while I had only been working with them for a few months, certain high ranking members (including the High Priest) began to seek my counsel on magical techniques as I had magical experiences that they themselves had never encountered in their traditional framework. This directly challenged my sense of learning and authority and I started to get the feeling that this was not the tradition for me. Life again intervened and I found myself heavily focused on mundane concerns, unable to attend more meetings with that group, so I practiced solitary once more.

Since I had become accustomed to people asking me about the Craft, I decided to put my experience to the test and began teaching public classes on my own. I found I was able to take my personal experiences and translate them for others so that they could benefit. I gained a deeper sense of self-confidence and control and generally found my calling as a teacher of the Craft. But something was still missing.

After a year or so I found what I was looking for; a local woman who was teaching a large group class in the Feri tradition. I signed up, paid my weekly tuition, and happily began to formally study the Craft. This was everything that I had hoped for: we were taught specific exercises, and had a space to share our experiences with those who had years of experience in the Craft. We worked with specific deities, spirits, and symbols of the tradition. Our work was slow… methodic… but could be spontaneous and at times even wild. I remember the first Feri ritual I went to… My friend (and later, husband) accompanied me to a Samhain gathering in Oakland, CA that was being offered by our teacher.

We were awestruck that everyone there (at least 30 or more) seemed to know the liturgical materials, and the power of everyone chanting them in unison was palpable. Though everyone had obviously memorized the same material it didn't seem "forced" or strained; these people had found a way to utilize traditional material in such a way as to allow it to inspire the power within them.

My reasons for wanting to formally study a tradition had largely to do with the fact that I was not the most disciplined person; in typical Piscean fashion I would skip ahead to the "cool parts" and leave the tedious and the "boring" for another day (which in all likelihood would never come). I knew that while I had learned a lot on my own that there were "holes" in my magical education and I wanted to be able to know with certainty that my training was complete and of value. I wanted more than just "book learning"; I wanted hands-on training overseen by someone who had been down that road before. I wanted it to count.

I studied for a few months with that Feri teacher, and while the material and workings were great, other life pressures meant that I was simply not in a space to commit to the class, and so I dropped out. I began circling with a local group who had wildly diverse backgrounds, including one who was an initiate of a Druidic tradition. We celebrated the Sabbats, honored the Full Moons, and generally celebrated life. I learned a lot, but it was still missing enough of a structure that I felt was necessary to establish a spiritual discipline.

A couple years later I found a teacher who finally 'clicked' with me, again an initiate of Feri. I trained with him for nearly 6 years before I received initiation; that crowning mark in our tradition that marks one's entrance to the priesthood.

Learning an established tradition was quite different than what I had experienced before. For starters, when I was on my own it was left up to me to decide the direction that my studies should take. Will I practice astral projection this week? Or shall I study the Tarot? In my Feri training there was a definite curriculum that we worked with. We began with basic ("tedious", "boring") exercises that would form a foundation; relaxation and concentration exercises that previously had held no interest for me, now suddenly given a context that made them appealing. We worked with specific deities; with specific exercises and symbols. I diligently studied with our little private group, attended weekly classes and the occasional ritual, and constantly worked with the material in ways that challenged many of the assumptions that I had made about myself and the Craft.

In the years prior to my traditional studies I had seen a segment of the Pagan population that seemed disinterested in discipline, seeming to favor fantasy over actual learning. In internet chatrooms everywhere "High Priests" and "High Priestesses" would emerge to share their wisdom, usually in the form of regurgitated materials that had come from the latest wave of popular books, which were themselves sometimes discredited or else given little value by those witches who learned their Craft in the context of coven and tradition. This growing trend was often a source of frustration to those who had studied "in the Old Way", and so these new "Johnny-come-lately's" were often the butt of jokes and the targets of scorn and ridicule. It was not uncommon for traditionally-minded witches to describe those who had learned the Craft outside of a coven as being "watered-down", "inferior", or to invoke a much used derogatory phrase, "fluffy bunny", common epitaphs even used perhaps by some in a manner that is "tongue-in-cheek", but are nevertheless in service of religious prejudice and zealotry.

Within in some traditional circles the mere suggestion of eclecticism is met with scorn. The example of those who "dig many shallow wells and never a deep one" is often cited as being an argument for focusing one's attention solely on a single path; to avoid confusions that may arise from conflicting belief systems, as well as to be able to fully master the particular material and work.

Some traditionalists believe that the inclusion of new ideas or practices dilutes or "contaminates" the traditional Craft. While this can indeed be true –consider the inclusion of Celtic or Germanic deities in an Egyptian ritual; while it is certainly possible that someone might legitimately argue for the validity of doing so, what can't be effectively argued is the existence of a historical tradition of doing so. It is absolutely more "traditional" to invoke Egyptian (and not Celtic or Germanic) deities in an Egyptian ritual, and so the inclusion of another culture's deities, myths, or symbolism alters the understanding of how the original religious system was intended to be experienced. Notice, however, that I have said nothing about the quality of such a ritual. While it is certainly not traditional to include another cultures deities, the argument that it should never be done is one that is born out of a sense of maintaining religious purity, and not of exploration or daring; qualities that I most definitely associate with the witch.

Where once the Craft was practiced in secret, that cat has been out of the bag for longer than I have been alive. Certainly there are covens and traditions that maintain some level of secrecy (and my own tradition is certainly among their number) but there are many, many more practitioners who have learned not in a coven, but from books, magazines, and public classes, and now even from websites, festival workshops, and online courses. This has given birth to a new generation of witchcraft; one in which the stringent attitudes of their more traditional forebears began to be thought of as "rigid", or "dogmatic"… and the practitioners themselves as "stuck-up", "egotistical", leading us back to "inferior".

What I have learned in the years I have been practicing the Craft is that both sides have it wrong. Each side claims superiority over the other, while ignoring the common thread that binds them both together. Traditionalists claim that they are practicing the "authentic" Craft and that eclectics –not having gone through the prescribed experiences— can never fully understand it; only the very specific practice or lineage afforded by the tradition is seen as being valid. Eclectics claim that traditionalists are living in the past, and that they are closing themselves off to further learning. It can be further argued that the "pure" (read: orthodox) traditionalist has lost the ability to be spontaneous and free; qualities much publicized by the Craft, modern and traditional alike.

Continued on page 56……

(1) This is how it was commonly spelled back then. Since our origin is as an oral tradition you can find this accurately spelled in many different ways; Faery, Fairy, Feri, Faerie, F(a)eri(e) being a few of the more popular spellings today. Victor Anderson began spelling it 'Feri' in the 1990's to help distinguish our path from others bearing similar names. Some people today refer to it as 'Anderson Feri tradition'.

When it comes to adaptability and spiritual practice, neo-Pagans are some of the most adaptable people out there. As a once popular bumper stick so boldly put it, "Where there's a Witch, there's a Way"; so it's no surprise that many modern Pagans have not only adapted to the Internet and technology but have flocked to it, embracing it with open arms. Today if you search the word "Pagan" in Google you receive 77,000,000 results. "Witchcraft" brings up close to 30,000,000 results while "Wicca" finds a little over 2.400,000 results. Wiccans, Witches, Pagans and Occultists have come to the Internet in large numbers to teach others, share their thoughts and ideas, dispel myths about who they are and connect with likeminded individuals.

In January 1997 a website called The Witches' Voice launched on the net. The site, which was created by Fritz Jung and Wren Walker out of their home, was started as an educational resource with their statement of purpose declaring them as a "proactive educational network providing news, information services and resources for and about Pagans, Heathens, Witches and Wiccans." At the time that the website started the Pagan presence on the net was just beginning to establish itself. In October of 1999 USA Today interviewed Fritz and Wren in an article titled "Witches find Web weaves practical magic in hunt for Believers" by Cesar G. Soriano in the Life section of the newspaper. In the article Fritz stated "We were clearly one of the few religious groups to embrace the Internet with a passion from the beginning," while further explaining that he felt the Internet was helping the Pagan community greatly, saying that before the Internet boom "we were very fragmented with no national communication. The Net blew this spiritual path wide open."

The Witches' Voice stands as a shining example of how the Internet has helped to grow and expand the Pagan community and allowed people reach out and find local covens and organizations as well as giving Pagans of all paths a place to share ideas and seek connections with others of like mind both on the Internet as well as face-to-face. When I talked to Fritz about the role of The Witches' Voice today he said "The Witches' Voice was designed to point Pagans from the net to local face to face groups and physical gatherings". Fritz adds that the site "is still an active resource for local networking today."

The Internet has become a vital outlet helping Pagans create a greater sense of community. Pagans from all around the world are now able to come together to work magick, learn, and share with those walking the same path or to find those with new and different perspectives to gain wisdom from. The Internet has changed the way Pagans get their news and information and how they come together offline as well, making it easier to find covens and learning circles where in the past it may have seemed as though there were none to be found.

Social Networking for Pagans

One of the more popular aspects of the Internet that has been largely embraced by the Pagan community is social networking. Mainstream sites like Facebook have a fairly large Pagan presence that continues to grow, offering a number of resources and outlets for Pagans. With the Groups feature on Facebook people have been able to create and find discussion areas of all sorts, allowing them to connect to people of specific paths or those in the general Pagan community. Many Pagan authors and community elders, covens, groves, shops, and public circles have groups and pages on Facebook allowing them to connect with Pagans and seekers around the world. With the ease of these kinds of interactions through Facebook it has made it so easy for people who have questions for their favorite Pagan authors and public figures to connect and get answers, where in the past you would have no real option other than sending a letter to the publisher or possibly an email to the publisher's website in hopes that it makes it's way to the author.

Some members of the community have found that Facebook alone has grown their fan base and follow ing in ways that working with their own websites and email groups haven't been able to for some time.

Starhawk commented on noticing this with her own Facebook page, saying "When I finally got myself a Facebook page I suddenly had more fans than I have on the Internet email list I'd been cultivating for years."

In 2005 a "do it yourself" social networking platform, The Ning Network launched allowing people to create their own social networks where the entire network could be focused around a specific interest, hobby, or cause. It was estimated that the number of individual networks hosted on Ning reached 1,000,000 in the spring of 2009. Many people in the Pagan community took to Ning to start Pagan social networks with specific tradition focuses or aimed at a specific geographical location, allowing Pagans and Witches to find others locally with even more ease. In the spring of 2010 Ning announced that it would no longer support free sites and would begin to charge network creators a monthly fee in order for them to host their networks. As a result many Pagan networks closed down or moved, but several large and notable Pagan focused networking sites remained in place and are still active today.

One of the most popular Pagan themed networks on Ning is PaganSpace.net. PaganSpace.net launched in October 2007 and has over 40,600 members and over 2,200 discussion groups. Anyone who is either a current magickal practitioner or who is just getting started and looking for a place to find others to chat with can be sure to find something of interest here. You'll even find some notable members here as well including Z. Budapest and Selena Fox. The popularity of PaganSpace has given way to Occult World Magazine, the official magazine of PaganSpace, and Labyrinth House Publishing, which announced in 2011 that it would be publishing a fiction series by Raymond Buckland.

For Pagans that live in an area such as the Bible Belt in the United States, it can be very difficult to seemingly impossible to meet and connect with other Pagans face to face. It can even be quite dangerous, in fact, for some to "come out of the broom closet" as we say, and therefore sites like this can be extremely important in helping to create a feeling of community. Being able to network on a site like PaganSpace where an individual can create a somewhat anonymous persona and while still being able to chat with others, participate in online classes and rituals, and get information on what is happening in the greater, global Pagan world. Websites like this can become a vital part of the life and path of some Pagans because it helps many to much less alone on their spiritual journey.

Does an online community create offline Community?

One concern that many in the physical community have had is that the vast amount of virtual community available for Pagans on the Internet has caused some of the face-to-face interaction to suffer. When asked about his view on this from his unique perspective, Fritz Jung from The Witches' Voice agrees that the Pagan community, as well as society as a whole, has seen declines with in-person groups interacting because of the amount of interaction taking place online. "Our society's social skills have atrophied in a big way; we don't interact physically like we used to." Even still, Fritz says that he does still feel today that the Internet played a part in helping the Pagan community come together and grow to where it is now. He points out that the most growth that the Pagan community saw as a result of online communication and sites like The Witches' Voice happened mostly from 1995 to 2005. In general Fritz feels that the growth of the Pagan community has somewhat slowed saying, "I believe the growth of the Pagan community in general flattened out 3-4 years ago." The Witches' Voice and other similar sites have seen a decline in traffic and activity he says, which he feels is due to the growth of sites like Facebook becoming the main way people of all walks of life, including Pagans, use as a key source for socializing, networking and promoting events and goods. Starhawk, who has been a leader in the Pagan movement for many years, offered some unique insights into how she's seen the Internet change and grow the overall community. The need arose to make changes and adjustments to embrace and grow with the Internet in order to reach more people in the community. In years past Reclaiming held a strict no photography or video recording policy at its events. As the Internet grew as way for Pagan groups to advertise their events, Starhawk realized that Reclaiming would need to make changes to these policies in order to promoteevents. "We now have limited photography and video at the Spiral Dance because we just couldn't promote it online without something visual."

"I think the internet has clearly given the whole Pagan movement a great boost as it has made information widely available that used to be very hard to find and secret," Starhawk said, adding that now if someone is looking for a coven or others to practice with that information is only a Google search away. And while she's found that her personal online presence has helped to fill offline classes and workshops it hasn't translated into an increase in book sales. Starhawk expressed concern for this area saying, "The online phenomenon has hurt publishing and made it extremely difficult to get books published, especially anything beyond Wicca 101." Realizing that more and more people were reaching out to the Internet for Pagan education Starhawk began teaching online, joining the ranks of other Pagan authors and leaders who have taken to the Internet to reach a wider audience, such as Z Budapest, Mara Freeman, T. Thorn Coyle, Raven and Stephanie Grimassi, and Janet Farrar and Gavin Bone. While this means having the ability to share knowledge and teachings with a wider and more diverse base of Pagans than before, Starhawk still says she prefers to work with people directly. "I personally would rather people get together face-to-face than online, but the Internet is certainly not going away!"

VIOLET FLAME GIFTS

CUSTOM OIL BLENDS

ALL NATURAL BATH AND BODY PRODUCTS

PURE ESSENTIAL OILS POURED TO SIZE

LARGE ARRAY OF STONES AND CRYSTALS

HAND MADE RITUAL ITEMS

CLASSES AND TAROT READINGS

740.349.3217

WWW.VIOLETFLAMEGIFTS.COM

ANGER
The Untamed Inner Flame

By Tim Titus

We love fire. Our society depends on it. Fire provides light and warmth. It transforms our food from inedible, and sometimes poisonous, to something delicious and nutritious. Of course, everyone knows that real fire must be carefully controlled. We could probably fill an entire magazine with horror stories of rituals that almost went horribly wrong because of a stray flame or a drooping robe that got too close to a quarter candle. We must carefully watch any flame we light.

But we also have a fire inside each of us. Our bodies are heated to 98.6 degrees. More esoterically, we all have a fiery passion that drives us and a will that fuels our magickal work. Every one of us has also felt the flaming heat of anger when someone did us wrong or hurt somebody we love. This inner fire provides energy that fuels our lives. Without it, we would be like a cold-blooded snake, lying inert on a rock as it tries to heat its body enough to hunt for food. However, just like physical fire, when the inner fire of anger is allowed free reign it can be just as destructive to our bodies and souls as any forest fire is to the beautiful trees it destroys along its voracious path, except it destroys us instead of trees.

It is so easy to let our anger run free. In many ways, anger's flame is harder to control than actual fire. We know what fire requires in order to burn: oxygen, fuel, and a spark. We know that taking away any of these or adding water will extinguish it. Rarely do people sit and stare at a raging fire and decide to let it burn freely, and they certainly don't throw gasoline onto it. We have a safety-driven, common sense understanding of how to control physical fires.

We aren't always quite so full of common sense when it comes to the fires that burn inside us, especially the intense heat of anger. Often, we do let our anger burn freely. We let it control us. It lingers in our minds. We hold grudges. We overreact to small provocations. We smolder over some small problem, which causes that problem to mushroom instead of devoting our actions toward a solution. While we promptly extinguish any fire outside of us, we actively throw deadwood onto the fires within us.

This is damaging to us, both as people and as witches. Physiologically, anger inflames the sympathetic nervous system. Our biological response to an angering stimulus is rapid heartbeat, shallow breathing, perspiration, flushed face, dilated pupils, and a spike of adrenaline. It's our body's typical reaction to all threats, which is why it has been nicknamed the "fight or flight" response (actually, it's now referred to as the "Four F's": Fighting, Fleeing, Feeding, and…well…Sex).

But, like everything else, our bodies need balance. When the fire of the sympathetic nervous system burns, it must take that energy from another system. In this case, it turns off the immune and digestive systems. So the more you let the fire within you rage out of control, the less fuel your stomach has to work properly and the less fuel your immune system has to protect you against disease. The result: ulcers and other gastrointestinal problems as well as increased vulnerability to sickness. Plus, all that pressure to keep your heart rate up leads to cardiac disease.

As if that wasn't enough, research shows that intense arousal can impair your ability to think. We've all made stupid decisions when angry. We've probably all come up with an obvious solution to a seemingly insurmountable problem after calming down and allowing ourselves to think about it rationally.

We do this because our minds are at optimum level when they are at medium temperature. The extreme heat of anger destroys our reasoning abilities. Instead of lighting the way, the flame of anger can blind us to reason. Between destroying your health and forcing unwise decisions, the uncontrolled fire within can damage you severely.

Uncontrolled anger can damage your craft as well. When fire rages within you, it lays waste to the balance of the other elements within you. If your anger is making your decisions for you, you lose sovereignty over yourself. You lose control of your own thoughts. You are controlled by the flames when you are supposed to control them. It's the inner equivalent of letting your campfire extend to the surrounding forest. What was helpful becomes harmful. Add to that the physiological inability to think straight while angry, and you have now unbalanced the Air within you as well as the Fire and Earth. Chances are you're not acting with love and compassion if you're driven by anger, so your inner Water is also evaporated as that fire continues to destroy your control over yourself. You are out of balance, unhealthy, and un-magickal.

Think of it this way. Your altar is a miniature representation of the universe. Tool correspondences vary, but let's just say that you have a pentacle for Earth, an athame for Air, a wand for Fire, and a chalice for Water. Allowing your anger to control your actions, imposing your rage-fueled will on your target whether through magickal or physical body blow, is like having a 50-lb. wand crushing your sacred work space while every other tool shrinks to the size of a thimble. As witches, we seek the balance of the elements within us and never want any one of them to overwhelm the others. We are our own altars; any lack of balance within us is reflected in our magick. Our magick is overwhelmed in the same conflagration that simultaneously burns away at our insides.

As within, so without.

It is so tempting to let that fire within us burn out of control. Someone angers us, and we just want to spew our flames all over them. In reality, that usually won't help. They usually just spew back, and both of us leave angrier than we were before with nothing solved. We can see this happen in our personal and family relationships, political activism, and quite often when we respond to the ever-growing discourse our society has online.

Our community has an extensive online presence. For the most part, it is a loving, supportive place. However, like in all families, arguments occur. The question is how do we deal with those disagreements? On a recent episode of Christian Day's Blog Talk Radio show, Hex Education, one of his guests referred to our all-too-common desire to scream and yell at each other online as "cyber balls." I think this is an appropriate description. We get indignant; we angrily defend our point of view. And we convince no one. We just stay angry. The fire stays inside our heads, hearts, and souls without any useful outlet. There's a reason that belittling, unproductive, troll-like angry comments are called "flaming." Cyber balls don't help anyone. They only fuel an out of control fire. And they burn you inside as well as out.

There are times when that fire is completely justified. Being passionate about an issue is good, and sometimes the target of your flames deserves the heat. That is when your control of the fire within as a witch becomes vitally important. If you let it rage on its own terms, you accomplish nothing and may even damage your own cause as your flames ravage everything in their path, destroying yourself while hurting others. Even worse, you may destroy your own cause through your uncontrolled anger. Go off the rails and people stop listening to you no matter how right you are. It's all the more tragic when you destroy a righteous cause through your unbalanced reaction. Thus, uncontrolled anger burns you, other people, and destroys the cause you fight for.

It may make you feel better, but it accomplishes nothing.

However, if like a fire tender at a ritual, you can channel and direct that inner flame into responses that reach just the right amount of heat, you have accessed the transforming power of Fire. Whether you do this magickally through spell work or through more conventional means is up to you. Too much heat will burn your dinner; just the right amount will make it awesome. Don't burn your magick; make it awesome.

Being a witch means having self control, even when faced with injustice. We work to manifest our will, not to spray it all over the place. Know your fire. Understand your anger. Stop and calmly assess where the fire of your reaction belongs. Before igniting out of control, direct your will onto a path that will cause actual transformation rather than one that just throws gas onto your inner blaze, making you feel better while accomplishing no actual change. A smith knows just the right amount of fire necessary to turn a hunk of iron into finely-wrought sword. Temper that fire with your mind and your heart to cause true transformation. You will be a healthier, happier, more successful witch.

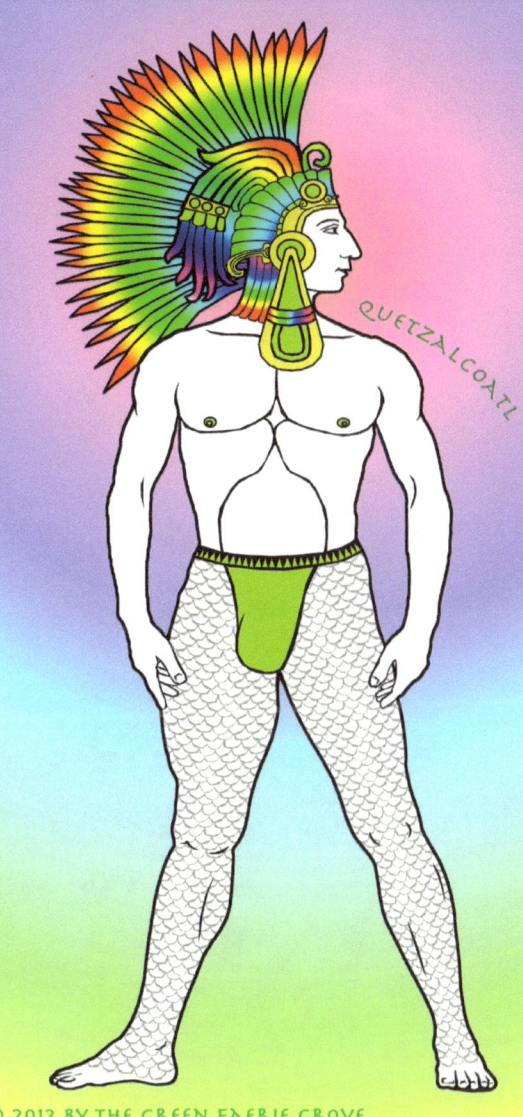

Between the Worlds
Men's Gathering

A Queer Pagan Brotherhood

September 10 – 15, 2012

In scenic southeastern Ohio

© 2012 by the Green Faerie Grove

Our 11th Year!

Registration begins March 1, 2012 and continues through August 17, 2012

For more information, please go to

www.betweentheworlds.org

Interview with a Fire Spinner

The Magical, The Fierce and The Brave.

Man has always been obsessed with fire. Civilization as we know it just simply would not be where we have found ourselves today without the discovery of the flame. As we live, work, and breath in a modern fast-paced world there are those who have chosen to follow the tribal roots of the sacred flame in the 21st century- the fire spinner.

Though we cannot accurately hone a date and place down for the origins of fire spinning we do know that people have been connecting to the sacred flame via this art form for thousands of years. In Bali the sacred fire dance originated from a trance ritual called the Sanghyang -a ritual that is reportedly performed to ward off evil witches and harm-doers. Though we don't know about evil witches, we do know that similar rituals were practiced in Celtic territories to ward off evil spirits.

In the 19th century fire spinning took a flying leap back into popular culture and left the world of forgotten tribal yesterday. Now fire spinning has become an integral part of tourist culture and now is being performed for tourists all over the world

Modern Witch Magazine sat down with professional fire spinner, teacher, and witch Soolah-Hoops to pick her brain about how fire spinning has effected her spiritual life. We figured if anyone would know what it was like to have a working relationship to fire- it would be her!
.

MW: What brought you to fire spinning?

S : I had seen fire poi dancing at festivals and was really drawn to it. Poi is a wick at the end of a chain and you usually dance with a set of two of them. The trails of fire it made in the dark of night created patterns and designs. I found it mesmerizing. The fire swirling around lit up the performer and shared an aspect of their beauty that you don't always see in people during the daylight hours. It was very magical to me. Afterwords, I bought a set of practice poi and tried using it but with it hitting me so much I just did not feel an affinity to it let alone felt good about possibly having balls of fire hit me in my face. I let it go for a few years. Then, at a festival, I saw a fire hoop and saw how the fire on it was in a more controlled form with spokes on the hoop. I thought, "Ok, I can do that!" and that is where it began. I practiced with regular hoops for a year and then on the anniversary of seeing the fire hoop I had my first burn. It was awesome! I kind of jumped right into it and it felt really natural to me. Because of the hoop and using mini hoops like poi I actually can do fire poi now.

MW: How do you feel fire spinning has affected your spirituality?

S: Each time I dance with fire I can feel how it sends me to a deeper realm. I can step into my hoop and light the wicks and it begins. The flames swirling around me, the whooshing sound, creating a vortex of light and heat, sits right inside my aura. I can feel it burning off the old. I can feel it transforming me from where I was moments ago to another place where my spirit is reflecting at a deeper level. When I spin fire I feel a connection to the heat of love of the universe, filling me up and then sending that energy out. It truly puts me in a place of being fully alive and in the moment each time I pick up a fire toy. I feel the energy of the spirits around me as well and a sense of everyone and everything shifting into realms beyond our every day. I feel our society really needs that at this time with all the shifting and tough changes happening in the world.

MW: How do you combine fire spinning and other magical/spiritual work?

S: I have actually cleansed fire circles and started ritual fires with my fire hoop. The heat of the fire and the sound of the flames as I spin I feel assists in shifting from one reality to another in creating ritual space.

MW: Do you work with any fire deities?

S: I haven't worked intentionally with any fire deities when it comes to day to day or to fire. I do feel I work with a lot of big Transformation energy though through Snake and my own personal deity the Goddess Medusa. They have shown up in images of me fire spinning. I sense an honoring of the aspect of transformation with fire not only within myself but I am sure it touches others as I do this. I honor fire and know it well. Each winter I am literally a hearth keeper at home. For years before the whole fire dancing thing, and to this day I, heat my home and do a lot of cooking with a wood stove in the winter. When you do that you have to sit with fire and you see the fire spirits dancing in the wood. It's right in your home all the time. You get up in the middle of the night to feed the fire and keep it going. You get burned at times doing this and you have no other choice but to honor it. I have more burn scars from tending the hearth than from fire spinning. It has its own sense of spirit. It guides and lets you know what you need to do next or gives you space to let go as the wood burns down into ash.

MW: When you do magical work how do you feel you depended connection to fire affects your work?

I feel for me that all elements are important to honor but my connection to fire is very deep. I have a different understanding of it. I see it in its birth stage as I set something aflame. I see it when it is full force with a roaring fire. I see it as it turns into quiet coals. Humans love to light ritual fires and dance ecstatically around it until dawn. I know in my heart that it speaks a different language. It has a different energy and life force than earth or air or water. Because I am a fire dancer it has made me fully aware that, with this honoring in the dance, I can work with it a lot easier than other elements. I am so deeply immersed in it a lot of the time that my connection improves the magical practices I do.

MW: What would you say is the most valuable lesson you have learned from spinning?

S: Fire spinning has taught me to break free of my fears and face them dead on. To allow for the full transformation of my being so that my passions in life can fully emerge. Sometimes taking risks will singe or even burn you but those warnings are part of the guidance fire brings. To not underestimate the size of the fire or the type of fire and its power. I did that in the past and then realized even the smallest flame can create a huge impact depending on how you work with it. Fire spinning has taught me that you have the ability to transform a moment in time to assist others to cross the everyday world. To stand on a different landscape and see that there is another world of possibilities that you may have not considered. It teaches me to share in igniting the light and passion within others to become ecstatic in their own way.

MW: There are a lot of witches out there who have a love/hate relationship with fire, any advice?

S: This question reminds me of my daughter when she would try to start the hearth fires at home. She's a Taurus and had struggled so much with fire. She'd sit for hours trying to get it started because she tended to let it go out if I was out of the house and then try to restart it instead of gently feeding it the whole time. "Oh thank God you are home! Mom, I am an Earth sign and Fire does not like me!!" But she had to sit with it and learn to understand it. It's like getting to know a person. It can take some time. Just be gentle with yourself if you have trouble with fire. Take small steps to create a loving relationship with it. Sit with fire. Start with something small like a candle or oil lamp and let fire know that you would like to find a way to bridge the personal gap that you have with it. In life we have close friends and acquaintances. Imagine turning an acquaintance into a close friend and the steps you have to take to make that change. You never rush into that relationship right? Feed the fire something lovely. Chocolate, honey, oranges or some other wonderful food item offered in a nice fire really gives it a different magical fuel. You feed your friends and acquaintances if you invite them to visit you, right? Do the same as you get to know fire. It might be time to reflect on you as well and why you feel this way about fire. Maybe you are afraid of the aspect of transformation. Maybe you are afraid of showing your deeper love or passions. You may be more of a passive energy than a fiery active one but fire can be passive as well in the slow burning coals and embers that sit below the active fires above it. Where deep within you does your spark sit when you are driven to actions that you do like to do? Sit and listen and see what it has to say to you. Some people will never have an affinity with fire and that is OK. You may just be called to work with other elements at this time but you can still honor it for its power and being. It brings you light. It keeps you warm in the winter. It cooks your food. It helps things to grow. It's all about the balance. Fire will love you gently as long as you are patient with it and take things at a good pace. I just want to end this with a lovely quote by Rumi that once you connect with fire you will see becomes true. "In each moment the fire rages, it will burn away a hundred veils. And carry you a thousand steps toward your goal."

Modern Witch Music

The Best of Sequoia Records

Meditation Drum
Dave and Steve Gordon/Sequoia Records

★★★★★

World Groove Mix Vol. 1
Various Artists/Sequoia Records

★★★★★

Celtic Lounge 3
Various Artists/Sequoia Records

★★★★

Buddha-Lounge 5
Various Artists/Sequoia Records

★★★★★

From the world of David and Steve Gordon - two legendary brothers in the ecstatic and electronic new age genre- comes Seqouia Records. Trust us, you know their work if you have ever tuned into Pagan Radio or any of the other spiritual/new age online stations. For 25 years Sequoia records has raised the bar of industry standard and have presented the pagan and witch community with the music that we meditate and dance to. In this first Modern Witch Magazine we pick the top Sequoia Records that every witch must have! Open your mind and take a deep breath these titles are the Modern Witch's Best of Seqouia Records.

David and Steve Gordon present what makes our best drumming album - Meditation Drum. We promise you this is not your mother's drum album. Four lengthy tracks guide us though Kundalini, Shamanic, and Empowerment drum stories. This album is the perfect compliment to your daily practice, Pranic work, and energy cultivation. This must have has everything we want from a drum album and gets a 5 out of 5.

I don't know about you but we love world music! In World Groove Mix Volume 1 Sequoia Groove unleashes beats from all over the planet that will have you mesmerized. This album doesn't sit on the self for long as it has become a go to for its hypnotic vocals and bewitching rhythms. No question about it- 5 out of 5.

For those of your witches out there who love Celtic music take a look at The Celtic Lounge III. The Celtic Lounge series has always been a favorite but their third and final addition tops the cake! Oh yeah, and I 2008 it won the COVR Record of the Year award. With artists like Gandalf and Everstar you cant go wrong! This Celtic treat gets a 4 out of 5.

Who hasn't heard of Buddha Lounge? Yeah that's what we thought! First released in 2002 the Buddha-Lounge series now boasts an impressive seven titles and we can't wait for number eight! This is the best thing to turn on and relax to after a busy day or to bring into your meditation regimen to spice up the visuals. Though I love the whole series my top pick would easily be Buddha- Lounge 5. Top of the line artists like TYA, Artemisia, and the Gordon Brothers give this collection a 4.5 out of 5.

The Witch's Tree
Continued

So, which path is correct? How can we practice a witchcraft that is effective and speaks to the needs of the moment, while retaining the wisdom of the past? What sort of model do we have that can help us hold onto what is good from our past, while still giving us the ability to grow into our individual and collective futures? The answer, at least for me, is in the trees.

A tree is a perfect symbol, in my opinion, for effective and authentic witchcraft. For starters, trees have long been associated with pre-Christian spirituality and magic, spawning an entire alphabet of magical language for the pre-Christian Celtic peoples, among others. Trees also have been seen as entrances to the Otherworld, as well as certain trees being used as temple spaces; sacred sites in which to better access and commune with spirit.

Trees are often used as symbols for the idea of different worlds that intersect our own. Consider the Kabbalah as the "Tree of Life", the Norse Yggdrasil, and the various other cultural expressions of "the World Tree". In this, the tree acts as an axis mundi; the connection between heaven and earth, or even the Three Worlds of the Angels and Stars (Overworld), the Ancestors and Faery (Underworld), and the realm of Humans and Animals (Middleworld). Consider the various types of experiences that are available in a magical system; those of traditional learning, discipline, and methodic work compared to inspiration, spontaneity, and innovation… all of which are important to effectively (and dare I say even traditionally) practice the Craft. The true purpose of witchcraft has always been to wield effective magic and only later to create a space of devotion for ones Gods. But these need not ever be in conflict with each other.

www.Faerywolf.com

I feel that my life experience has been invaluable in that I have benefitted from many types of Craft training and experience and --with the perspective that nearly 3 decades of practicing witchcraft has afforded me—I can now definitively say that all of the aforementioned approaches to the Craft have their place and indeed each have something to offer the seasoned practitioner by way of underscoring the necessity of both traditional wisdom as well as exploration and experimentation.

The symbolism of the tree reflects that experience in that my roots hold steadfast as my foundation and reflects the traditional training I received and my early personal experiences. All else flows from this foundation, but nothing is restrained by it any more than the roots of a tree restrain the growing of its trunk and branches. As in the invocation that began this essay, the four roads meet at this tree, representing the powers of the physical elements. But these are also the components of a type of "complete witchcraft" that draws together many divergent threads of various types of witchcraft into a cohesive whole; the crossroads marking the spot where the prayers are made, where the magic is done, where the tree of the world connects the infernal with the heavenly. In the east, the place of air and of dawn, we find information and the communication of knowledge. This is the element of the written and spoken word, as well as the path of teaching and of learning; of acquiring and sharing of knowledge. Here is the place of study in its many forms including that provided by books, websites, and the like. In the south, the place of fire and noon, we find the warrior spirit; the honing of our sharpened will. Here, through the fires of life experience, we learn how to put our gathered knowledge into action; and how to generate the power necessary to see our actions through. This is the path of magic and sorcery, of causing transformation and change. In the west, the place of water and dusk, we find our daring or passion. Here we also find the depth of our connection to each other, as all rivers flow into the sea. Here we also find cleansing and healing, as well as visions and dreams; divination, astral travel, and shamanic journeying fulfill this path. In the north, the place of earth and midnight, we find the powers of death and the ancestors; the wisdom of the traditional Craft and the "Old Ways". Here we are reminded of the secrecy and how keeping this practice alive can connect us to the mysteries and powers of ancestral witchcraft. This path is that of the necromancer; those who work with spirits and the Mighty Dead. Together they remind us that the real power of the Craft occurs when all four roads meet in the center, "between the worlds", where the world tree grows.

Those branches of various practices stem from the central trunk and burst into leaf, flower, and fruit; things that are very different than the roots that hold it secure in the earth, and provide very different and very necessary functions for the tree as a whole: providing nourishment to our Craft in the form of new ideas, art, myths, and the ability to offer that nourishment to the world.

The system that forms the roots is the very same that forms the trunk and branches; each year growing in thickness, forming rings and expanding outward. This growth cycle can be seen as our collective Craft, with tradition at the heart of our magical understanding, forming the basis for our ever expanding knowledge and practice. Consider that the vast majority of those who call themselves 'witches' (and yes, even 'warlocks') today are at the very least familiar with 'Casting a Circle', whether or not they are able to perform it in a traditional way; thus traditional knowledge has been handed down as a basic magical 'meme' which carries the seed of the magic outward into the airs of communication and change.

while at the same time must also be able to retain their basic structure in order to be recognizable. Though they share some commonalities, I'm sure everyone would agree that a tree is different from a vine.

In my view, the Craft is a wild fruit-bearing tree that holds true to the Old Mysteries, and grows unabashedly into the light of the future, offering the world new food to fill their bellies. As Feri founder Victor Anderson said (2), "Our Pagan community is growing and showing much bright promise. The Craft is a tough weed that will grow many strange flowers and bear strange fruits, so we must try and tolerate different ways of practicing it. Learn from what we see and if we cannot use it, let the others try, even if they eat bad fruit and go balls up!" The drive of the Craft has always been to create… to innovate… to address the changing needs of the moment. Often this derives from the wisdom of our ancestors. But just as often we are asked to adjust our practice with the inclusion of new knowledge… new ideas… new magic. To do otherwise is to allow our magic to become dogmatic and stagnant. Tradition cannot be allowed to become the enemy of the exploration necessary to the discovery of new knowledge. And innovation cannot be allowed to disconnect us from our past. The branches cannot supersede the needs of the roots, nor can the roots usurp the needs of the branches; both are needed to make the system work. Either extreme makes for a very unhealthy tree. When in balance, the process is nothing short of the miracle of life. If we are to claim the power of the witches' fire, we must be prepared to really look at all the ways and paths of magic that are around us. There are many ways to tap into the power.

(2) Victor Anderson, Green Egg, Vol. XXVI, No. 100, Spring 1993

> *The Craft is a tough weed that will grow many strange flowers and bear strange fruits, so we must try and tolerate different ways of practicing it.*
> *–Victor Anderson*

As we move further into the 21st century we are being asked to adapt to new ways of life, while keeping a link to our past. The work I embody is to do just that; to maintain the traditional wisdom while retaining also that original sense of exploration and experimentation so vital to our continued growth. Our job as practitioners of the Craft is not simply to regurgitate what we have been taught by our teachers. Our true job is to take what we have learned and then move outward, expanding our knowledge. We must not worship our teachers. We must honor them. And to do this best we must become stronger, better, wiser. Only when we surpass our teachers does the Craft truly grow. Like parents who want better lives for their children, we must do what is best to pass on our values as well as a sense of daring and courage to move beyond the boundaries of convention and embrace that divine fire of inspiration and magic; strengthening our Craft… shaping our future.

Modern Witch PODCAST

If you like Modern Witch Magazine, You'll LOVE The Modern Witch Podcast.

Music, News, Reviews and Pagan Pop-culture for the Modern Witch

www.themodernwitchpodcast.com

The Inner Mounting Flame

Why internal work is important

By Taylor Ellwood

If I have one complaint about Western Magical systems, it's the lack of focus on internal work. Instead the focus is on doing a spell to get a result or to change the environment around you. The problem with such an approach is that it's extremely short-sighted, because it doesn't take into account the internal changes that need to occur. The average spell book is a recipe book designed to help you cook up a result, but it doesn't tell you how to keep that result, or deal with the consequences. It's all left up in the air. To cultivate the internal flame of your inspiration and creativity and to generate results that are sustainable and maintainable, the focus needs to shift toward internal work.

What is internal work? It's meditation, internal alchemy, and the cultivation of chi. Actually those are just techniques. Internal work is the ability to work with your values, beliefs, emotions, internal energy, and internal reality, with the understanding that the cultivation of your internal reality leads to changes within your external reality. The

reason for this is simple. Your values and beliefs shape your attitude and approach toward life and yourself. They determine if you will keep that result you want, or if it'll be sabotaged by some part of yourself that doesn't want it. Let me provide an illustrative example. In my early twenties, I found myself attracted to girls that I knew wouldThe always reject me. My reasoning for trying to get involved with such a person was that I genuinely believed that I didn't deserve to be with anyone. This didn't change until I did internal work that helped me work through my limiting beliefs and enabled me to realize I did deserve to be with someone who genuinely liked me. I continually sabotaged myself until I did the internal work. The internal flame of your being, your inner spark or muse, is something that must be cultivated through self knowledge and conscious awareness.

I discovered internal work when I began practicing Taoist and Buddhist meditation techniques. The focus of those techniques involved not only exploring my internal reality, but also integrating my body into the exploration of that reality. Thus, I ended up doing not only breathing meditation, but also moving meditation, all of which provided a holistic approach to internal work. Such an approach recognizes that the physical tension and stress the body experiences can be symptomatic of emotional and mental stress that a person has repressed(1).

One of the techniques I use on a daily basis is a Taoist breathing technique called water breathing meditation. As the meditator inhales, s/he draws the internal energy from his/her belly and moves it to the top of his/her head. As s/he exhales, that energy is released to go down into the body and dissolve any blockages that are encountered. The dissolving process is not a forceful one. You don't want to break internal blockages. Instead you want to massage them, melt them, and gradually pull them apart. The resultant release of tension frees internal energy that has been constricted by the tension. It also releases emotions and provides the person an opportunity to work with those emotions and resolve the actual issues that caused the tension.

This is just one example of internal work. Internal work necessarily involves working through the issues within your life so that you can release yourself from toxic beliefs and values that would otherwise hold you back. Not surprisingly, if you consistently do some form of internal work in your daily magic practice, the need to do more overt forms of magic significantly lessens. The reason is simple: By working through your internal issues and resolving any contradictions that work against you, life becomes easier to live. Events line up in your favor because you are actually embodying what it is you need to manifest. The need to do more overt forms of magic is no longer as necessary because you are no longer sabotaging yourself. You become your greatest agent of change. You will still need to do magic on occasion to stack the deck in your favor, but in such cases, you'll find it much easier to obtain the result because you will truly know what you want.

The inner mounting flame of your soul will align with the innermost desires of your mind, and the water of your emotions, to fully take form in your body, and in the expression of your life.

(1) But physical stress can also be symptomatic of other physical issues in the body as well!

SITTING YOUR ALTAR

BY HEATHER KILLEN

Despite the great grey beast of February rearing its head, spring is indeed here in its seedling state. Imbolg; fire, candles, bread, corn dollies, lambs, and the first twitching of spring are the classic images that pop to mind. The waxing of sunlight is celebrated with fire. But, light does not overthrow dark until the heartbeats after the spring equinox. We are at the waxing nightlight glow that Nature has given us to see by. We are in the darkness of spring.

There is a core principle called in different communities, 'Sitting your Altar'. Sitting your Altar more often than not includes silence. The ability to sit, listen and truly hear, as best to your growing perception, where you need to focus, where and how you need to move, what is coming at you, what personal behaviors/modes of operation truly do not serve you, what needs to change, what needs to stay and be nurtured and what needs to be ripped out.

It is personal inventory and gut check time with input from your honorable ancestors, Deities, spiritual and natural allies. It is a wakeful trace that brings renewed and expanded clarity.

The altar is a psychological trigger. A touch stone, the place of center, the meeting place on many levels. We are working with the internal altar when we tell someone to sit their altar. How you personally access this will vary. The key here is to trigger your spiritual awareness and shift the consciousness and perception. Sitting in front of your altar with incense and a few candles, or in front of a sacred fire, or spinning on drop spindle (a personal trance and listening favorite), whatever works and what is most appropriate for you personally.

This is a simple process that many have difficulty with. Some practitioners have the inclination to over complicate this process. That is a focus issue and stalling tactic that needs to be addressed and overcome.

Sitting your altar makes you face yourself, for those who are uncomfortable with that, well, that's an issue this practice can help with. If you actively work to embrace your shadow and keep your shadow closet cleared and organized, it is easier to sit silently with yourself and be honest with yourself; it enables awareness and perception to grow. With a clear channel we can hear and perceive better because that's what this does. The Toltec called it a 'shifting of the assemblage point', and working with the "Island of Tonal". Changing where your focus is looking and listening, while others may call it moving into a Hanged Man position to perceive and gain clarity from a different angle.

So, what are some first steps that can be used to start sitting your altar? Well, your altar of course. Maintaining an altar is work; anyone telling you otherwise is not being honest. If you are using the altar actively then there's going to be candle wax drippings, incense left overs, various herbs, stones, food and drink offerings being moved in and out, changing the altar cloth, etc. If you don't already have a permanent altar set-up, it's time to get creative and get to work. If you do have a permanent altar set up, chances are it's time to tidy it up a bit. Altars do not have to be elaborate. Keeping things simple helps keep energies and thoughts focused. The top of a dresser, a small plant stand in the corner, a shelf, (you know this, you've been told this, no more excuses).

The altar needs to be someplace where you will see it frequently. Seeing the altar will trigger the subconscious, seeing a candle and incense burning on an altar, even more so. As we work and maintain the altar we are reminded that we need to tidy, bolster, maintain our inner Spiritual core and check in with our true selves and Spiritual Allies. This is where the eureka moments happen. We sit the altar as cleansing and centering. We sit the altar to problem solve and manifest what we need.

How to Work with Sitting Your Altar

If these things are not already on your altar gather: purification incense, a candle, small dish of salt, and a small chalice of water. Dim the lights in the space you are working in. Sit before your altar; look at every item on it. Why is each item there and how do their magicks weave together. If there is an object that is on the altar but is out of harmony, really look at it. What does it represent? What corresponding vibration within yourself might you need to look at?

Light sage or your favored purification incense. Give yourself a good wipe down smudging. Feel the stresses and worries of the day slipping away, quieting down and losing their emotional edge. The loud internal dialogue and judge/justification voice must be ball-gagged.

It may still muffle, but the focus is now being shifted and it's officially in time out for a bit. This is soul time. For those who are highly visual, sualize a golden ball gag on your internal loudness so you can listen better. Place the incense back on the altar.

Next, light the candle. The color of the candle should be in correspondence with your work. Why have you come to the altar? (Some examples of color and purpose could include: white: purification, protection, any need; black: protection, shadow work; green: finances and money issues; blue: healing; violet: clarity, purification, psychic ability; red: passion, acceleration) Lightly gaze at the candle. Keeping your focus in mind… why did you come to the altar? To trouble shoot a curve ball life threw at you? To purify? For clarity? How a challenge or need may be met? To deal with a personal trauma? Need guidance?

Ask for the aid of your guides, guardians, honorable ancestors, Goddess and God. Dropping down into light trance, listen, watch, feel, smell, go inside yourself. Sit there in that way, in that open and listening space. Watch as the realm of possibility opens wider. Seeing and sensing the focus from different angles and vibrations. You will know when to come back to full consciousness. You will feel it and come back naturally, or be interrupted (it happens sometimes).

Place a pinch of salt on your tongue, centering and receiving the blessings of health, prosperity, and protection. Next, sip from the chalice of water. Washing, cleansing, moisturizing and nourishing your body on all levels.

Journaling is highly encouraged. Keep track of what you feel, see, and sense during your altar time. Looking at dates, weather, moon phase, days of the week, etc. can also help identify challenging periods of our personal wheel of the year. Once we become aware of a pattern we can look at it closer and see if it's fine or if it needs to shift it's vibration to something more healthy and needful for ourselves and our families. Keeping a magickal journal will help you identify your own patterns.

An interesting thing happens as we sit our altar regularly. Our personal vibration changes, it strengthens, becomes more refined, focused and at peace. Our clarity grows. The ability to raise, focus and release energies increase. Why? Because we're clearing out the debris from inside allowing for better flow and gentle strengthening of the inner channel. We are becoming a better hollow bone. Because your vibration will brighten and strengthen keep in mind the principle of forced resonance.

Cycles, jobs, relationships, things that no longer serve your highest good will be forced to change or be removed from your daily life. That doesn't mean that what leaves is necessarily a bad thing, just stuck in a particular vibration or needing to go in a different direction for their own personal growth. This is what I call the Five of Cups effect. Your energetic dead ends are going to be trimmed so new growth and bounty can grow for you. Doreen Vailente wrote the truth with the words "…If that which you seek you find not within, you will never find it without…" It is the fire within, the Divine spark of Spirit that we are accessing and working with. It can be seen as a forge that burns inside your deep heart. All forges need to be tended to operate correctly, all forge fires need stoked from time to time, they need air, and they need fuel. What type of fuel are you putting in your forge? Is it time to stoke the coals? Are you allowing the air and inspiration from your Deities, guides, guardians, honorable ancestors and omens to blow across the fire or do you have the damper sealed and the door shut? Is your forge bright and hot and producing? Actively nurture your inner fire to grow in health, strength, awareness, wisdom and authentic power. No one else can do this for you. Like the story of Vasalisa, you must go through the dark woods alone, work hard and bring back the fire and light.

Modern Witch EXCLUSIVE

Within the Cards
By Rowan Pendragon

Chapter Sampler

Within The Cards
Using Knowledge and Psychic Vision to Read the Tarot

ROWAN PENDRAGON

In September 2011 Rowan Pendragon released her first tarot book titled "Within The Cards". Rowan has over 25 years experience working with and reading tarot. She is a certified tarot consultant, among many other magickal and metaphysical certifications, many of which she works into her tarot practice. "Within the Cards" was written at first as a small class manual for teaching her tarot intensive but then grew into the 330 page first edition that is currently available.

"Within the Cards" is a focused on tarot reading techniques for both beginners and seasoned readers who are interested in developing their psychic skills while learning the read the cards with the use of traditional tarot knowledge. The book explores the concepts of the Tree of Life with the tarot, how to identify personalities in the court cards to make reading them easier, and number of psychic development and reading techniques to help you grow your tarot practice.

In the chapter "Working with the Sight", Rowan presents her technique for using various psychic skills to get the most out of each card in a reading. In this chapter she shares exercises for working to develop these skills and then how to use them specifically in a reading. As well as exploring these steps in depth, she presents a short list of the five key psychic steps for reading tarot as part of a technique she calls the Tarot Detective Method.

Five Psychic Steps for Reading Tarot

1. Visualization (Stepping through the window) – See yourself walking through the card as though it were a doorway or window that brings you directly into the scene pictured in the card.

2. Seeing (Clairvoyance) – Looking at the image in the card, allow your mind's eye to view the scene without judgment, letting any images that need to get your attention jump out at you or come to life.

3. Knowing (Claircognizance) – When you are looking through your cards in a reading allow yourself to go with any gut feelings you have about the meanings of a card regardless of whatever keywords or meanings you may normally attribute to a card. Allow this sense to also draw you to specific cards that may need extra attention.

4. Hearing (Clairaudience) – Once you have stepped into a card listen to things people may be saying within the image or listen for any sounds in the environment within the card as well as in your own physical environment while reading as they can be triggers to confirm something you are picking up.

5. Feeling (Clairsentience) – Allow yourself to get an overall sense of the layout of the cards in a reading based on how you feel when you initially lay out the cards. Also, when you step into a card, sense how you feel while in that environment and determine what emotions are brought up for by that card.

In the chapter "Seeing the Details", a chapter which looks specifically at the minor arcana, Rowan presents the idea that each suit in the minor arcana tells it's own story within the larger story of the tarot. To illustrate this, she takes that cards of the suit of wands and uses them to tell a story and then provides some guidelines for the reader to do the same thing as an exercise with one of the other suits. Below is this excerpt entitled "The Tale of Ten Wands".

A spark, a thought, a creation; everything began with an idea and a dream and the realization that anything is possible if one is willing to seize control and power in their own lives. At least that's how the story started out for Edward. (Ace of Wands) Edward grew up in a castle, which overlooked the ocean. As he grew up living his days in this remove seaside village, Edward began to get restless and started to daydream about what else might be out in the world for him. He'd never left him hometown and didn't know if the stories he'd grown up on were true. He would stand atop the parapet of his home, looking out at the ocean dreaming, contemplating, and wondering about what could be. (Two of Wands)

As the years carried on, Edward grew even more restless and one day, while standing on the edge of the rocks overlooking where the ships came to port, he decided it was time to go out and find adventure. (Three of Wands) After announcing to his friends and family that he was ready to venture away from home they threw a lavish party for him to celebrate what would surely be a wonderful time for him. Edward knew as he stood looking back at his parents who waved at him as he left, that he would come back one day as a man they could be so proud of. (Four of Wands)

Edward found a group of other boys and young men who were seeking adventure and they spent their time together developing their battle skills, learning how to fight and work with weapons. Edward learned a lot about dealing with others his own age during that time and learned about the power of competition. He'd never had to deal with this before and he learned so much about himself during that time. (Five of Wands) After a handful of years away, and having fought several battles with success, it was time for Edward to return home. He'd had his adventure and he'd been victorious, proved what he felt he needed to prove to those around him, and now he was on his way back to his seaside village. Never did he imagine that his return would be full of so much celebration and fanfare! It was in that moment, as he crossed the threshold he'd previously waved farewell through years ago, that he sat up taller on his horse with more pride and realized that he would need to take time to adjust to life in the village again. Edward also knew deep in his heart that he now had a responsibility to those he would be among to guard them and protect them. (Six of Wands)

One morning there was a loud noise coming from the shore that startled Edward from his sleep. Immediately he was reminded of his silent oath he took to defend his home and the people of his village so he sprang into action, throwing on whatever clothes and shoes were within arms reach. He grabbed his wand and ran to the edge of the cliff at his home, ready to defend against the intruders who were slowing making their way up the cliff face. (Seven of Wands) Edward worked hard to defend the village that day but all his battle skills came rushing back to him as though he'd never put down his wand in the first place. He battled and was quick to run off the enemies that would have come to ravish the small village. As a sign that all was well and that everyone was safe, Edward flung the wands of those he defeated through the air from the clifftop and toward the village. He did this to send a message; no one shall defeat him and he shall always keep the village safe. This news left everyone to let out a sigh of relief and they had hope that they would never need to worry about intruders again. (Eight of Wands)

As time went on, Edward continued to defend the village and he worked nonstop to ensure that everyone was safe. Edward was seen as one of the most treasured guards of the villages and his endurance and stamina were shown in his willingness to go to great lengths to keep watch on everyone around him. Even though he knew this was his calling and what he needed to do, Edward began to grow tired and this caused him to get overly defensive when someone would comment on his work or efforts. Edward knew it was almost time for him to give up his post. (Nine of Wands)

Then, one day, after so many years of holding this position in the village, Edward decided it was time to leave and go home to rest for good. Edward gathered together his wands and his trophies from all his hard work, including the wands of those he'd defeated in his battles, and prepared to leave. As he made the journey back to the castle of his family, his back began to hurt and he started to walk hunched over from the weight of his load. Edward stopped for a moment to rest and realized just how much he'd been doing for others for all these years and how now, at a moment where he could have used someone to come to his aide, there was no one there to help him. While Edward held no regrets for his years of service, he knew that he was making the right choice and that it was time for him to go home and release his burden. (Ten of Wands)

In Chapter 10, "Reading With Honor", Rowan discusses the sometimes tricky topic of ethics with tarot reading and some of the situations that you may encounter while reading for others. Rowan shares a lot of her personal thoughts on ethics with regard to tarot including the occasion where a reader may need to say no to a client.

Knowing When To Say NO To A Client

There are going to be times that your ethics will be tested when doing readings.
Quite often the challenge will come with the type of reading or the question that someone presents to you. Something that I have encountered a great deal with my phone line clients is what I call "psychic spying"; it's when someone wants you to do a reading for them to find out what someone else is thinking or doing. This is common when people want to know about a relationship issue and they want to know what the other person really thinks of them or if they are really interested in them.

While this can seem like a perfectly legitimate and valid question, think for a moment about what this person is really asking. They are essentially asking you to psychically pry into the mind of another and read their personal, private thoughts. Would you want someone to do that to you? Probably not, so it's best not to do it to someone else. When I find myself faced with these questions I always remind the client that the reading is for them and should be about them and not a third party who isn't present to give their consent to the reading.

When faced with these sorts of questions it isn't a bad idea to ask the person why it is that they don't know this; is there a reason they don't feel comfortable asking the other person these questions? Chances are they are just frightened and scared of being rejected but this isn't a reason to do this sort of work. Instead you might want to do a reading to find out if there are reasons for them to be worried about such things or how they can strengthen their bond with this other person so that they can ask such questions.

With these clients I also stop to think about the responsibility aspect for the client. Why can't this person be comfortable with asking their partner these questions? Often this is where I take the reading and we end up looking at the underlying reasons about why the client can't be open with their partner. This ends up revealing far more useful and actionable information for later. Saying no to a client also becomes a factor when a client becomes somewhat addicted to readings. Keeping in mind that reading is a process of energy exchange it can become difficult to keep this going over and over again on a daily or weekly basis with the same person. No matter how hard you try you may very well find yourself in a position where you're taking on some of the problems or issues of your client because your energy is becoming so entwined.

Again, don't be ashamed or afraid of referring a client to another reader and don't feel like you're rejecting them when you tell them that you don't feel it's a good idea for you to read for them again on a question that you've addressed with a handful of readings already. When you do a reading about the same question over and over, ultimately seeking a different answer, you can begin to put energy into that situation that can become confusing. That energy can ultimately effect that situation and make things more complicated.

When you have someone asking for readings about the same things again and again, or you have someone that is coming to you for readings with high frequency, basically getting readings for every little decision they need to make, it's time for them to take a vacation from readings for a little while. You'll want to be as gentle and diplomatic as possible in this situation, but you do need to be firm. Let me know that even if you did a daily reading for them they still need to make the decisions that drive their actions and their lives. This can also be a good time to reinforce the idea that no readings are set in stone and that all actions and decisions that they make determine the true outcome of a reading; you are just a guide not the driver.

"Within The Cards" by Rowan Pendragon can be purchased through Amazon.com or directly from Rowan through her online shop. You can find "Within The Cards" in paperback and digital editions.

Rowan is also available for private tarot readings, angel card readings, coaching, and magickal consultations.

Visit www.onewitchsway.com or www.rowanpendragon.com for more details.

What do you see when you read the cards?

Memorization is the way that many of us start reading the tarot, but true tarot reading is more than just repeating meanings from a book.

"**Within the Cards**" by Rowan Pendragon explores the psychic developement side of tarot reading as well creating keywords for the cards through interpreting the colors , images, and symbols in the cards.

Topics covered include:
The basics of the major, minor, and royal arcanas
The Tree of Life and the tarot
Psychic development
Reading with psychic sight
Asking effective questions
Creating your own spreads
Starting a tarot business
Tarot spells
Tarot journaling
Tarot meditation

$24.99 - 330 pages - 7.44" x 9.69"
ISBN-13: 978-1466310742

Available through Amazon.com
Visit www.rowanpendragon.com for more details.

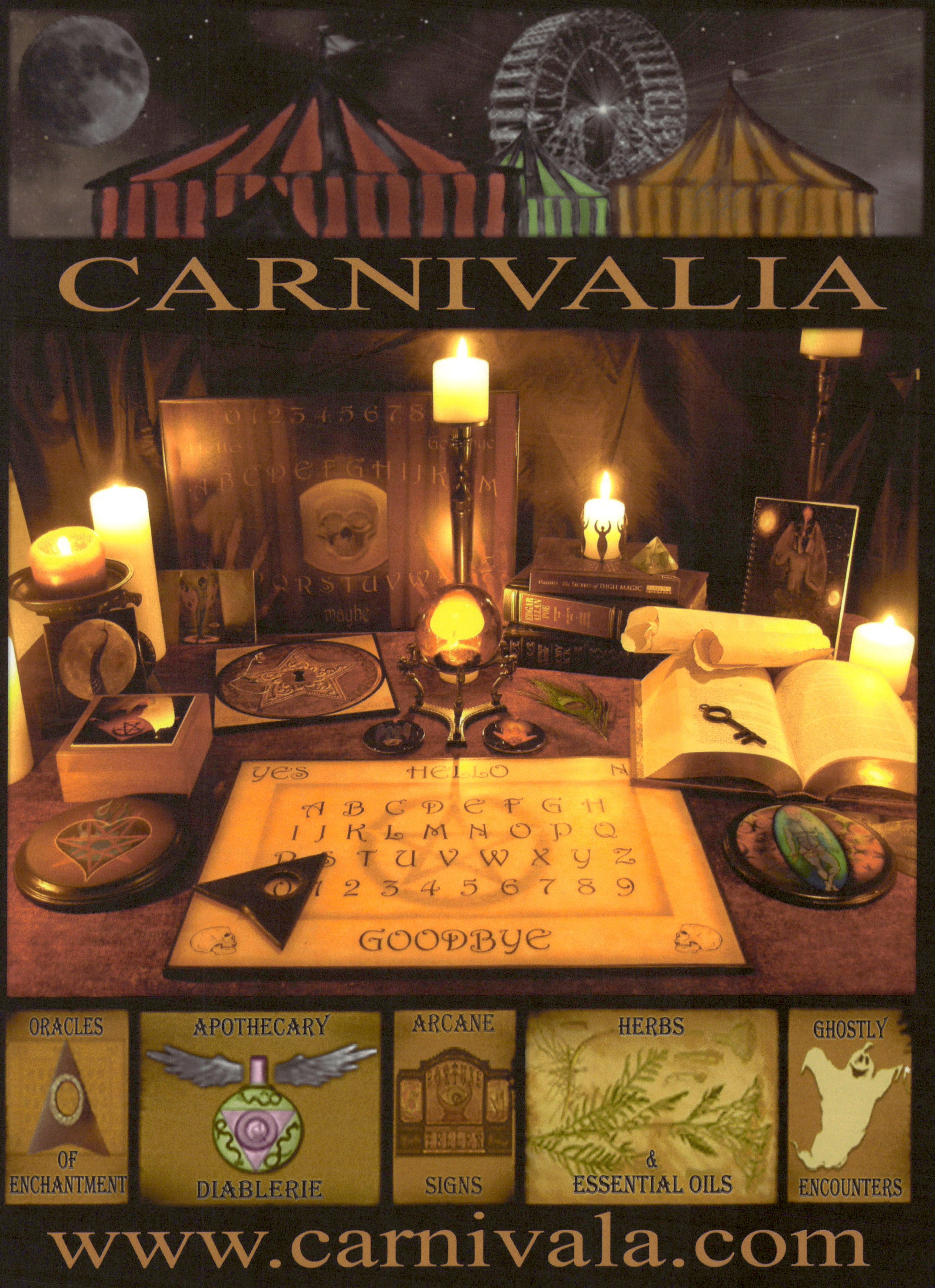

CARNIVALIA

ORACLES 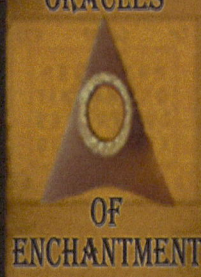 OF ENCHANTMENT	APOTHECARY  DIABLERIE	ARCANE  SIGNS	HERBS  & ESSENTIAL OILS	GHOSTLY  ENCOUNTERS

www.carnivala.com

During the early part of 2010 I had begun a journey to explore various aspects of shamanic work more. I was just wrapping up my first year studying the Temple of Witchcraft tradition and were we getting ready to move on to Second Degree I was already thinking ahead to Third Degree. In The Temple of Witchcraft tradition there are Five Degrees to work through and the Third Degree is focused on the shamanic side of Witchcraft. This was the material I was really looking forward to working with the First and Second Degree classes and material was largely going to be review for me. I began reading more book on various forms of shamanism, started to work with a number of shamanic meditation techniques, and started to look for more opportunities to learn all I could.

I had begun attending a shamanic woman's circle and met a few shamanic teachers and practitioners. That summer one of these teachers was starting a new round of classes on shamanic journeying and I thought this would be a great opportunity to get a jump on things for the future. We were already working with some pretty solid meditation techniques with the Temple Degrees and I was very happy with where those practices were going, but I was ready for a bit of a challenge.

As it would turn out the classes didn't yield a lot of results for me. I didn't care for the teacher or her teaching methods. We clashed several times, including once on my interpretation of one of my journeys where she insisted I was wrong. Through my own perception, hearing some of the things this teacher talked about in class, and many of the examples of things that she gave for journeys and interpretations, it was clear to me that she had much of her own healing still to do.

There was one thing that I took away from the class, a practice that turned out to be something we learned on the very first day and was the one thing that stuck with me. I have modified this a little to suit my own practice.

It is a process of cleansing and releasing through something my teacher called Fire Ceremony, a small cleansing ritual done in container that uses the power of fire to burn away negative attachments and negative energies. It is a process of transformation through the fire that can release energy patterns in order to allow new ones to develop in their place.

To do this you'll need the following:

A small incense cauldron
A tile or trivet for under the cauldron
Epsom salts
91% proof alcohol
Small strips of parchment (leaves of sage can also be used)
A pen
Long lighter or long matches
A small offering

Because this is a mini ritual that deals directly with negative energies and entities, it is highly advised to perform this rite either within a cast circle for with a certain level of protections set in place. In the shamanic practice I learned this in, this involved calling in spirit animals and energies of the four directions as well as calling in the powers of earth and sky. It's also a good idea that for this work you have a spirit guide or ancestor called on to be with you to keep you safe. Unleashing these negative energies has the potential of causing a little trouble for some so it's good to err on the side of caution.

Now you can set up your cauldron. Place the cauldron on the tile and fill the bottom with about a half-inch of Epsom salts. The alcohol needs to be 91% alcohol or higher; lower concentrations do not burn as well or you need a lot more to get a proper burn. You can find rubbing alcohol at this volume in some drug stores but you can find it fairly easily at medical supply stores.

Add about 2 tablespoons of alcohol over the salts. You want to be careful to not add too much but you also want to make sure you have enough to make the fire burn well. You absolutely should not add more alcohol after having lit the fire. This can be extremely dangerous and cause a burst of flame and create a fire outside of your cauldron and likely catch you on fire! So be sure to add what you need at the beginning. Next you need to set your intention. Decide what it is that you really need to release, and be sure you're ready to release it! Many times we might way we're ready to be free of something but when those things are removed from us we feel a sense of loss and regret. Be sure your intentions are clear and true. Once you know exactly what it is that you want to release you can begin to write them on your slips of paper. One side of the paper is going to have what you want to release and the other will have what you want to have come to you in its place. Try to focus on only one or two things at a time so you can give them your full attention. Write them down either in a few words or as a larger statement.

For example:
"Impatience"
or
"I release my impatience with others."

On the other side of the paper write what you want to transform this into. In this cast it might be:

"Patience"
or
"I receive the gift of patience in my life." or *"I have patience with those around me."*

After writing your papers you need to breathe into them by reading your paper. Hold up your paper and blow onto the side of what you want to release and then read aloud what you wrote. Then turn the paper over, breathe on the side and read what you wrote.

Now use your lighter or matches to light your fire. Once your fire is lit throw the paper into the flame and watch it burn. As the fire burns use your hands

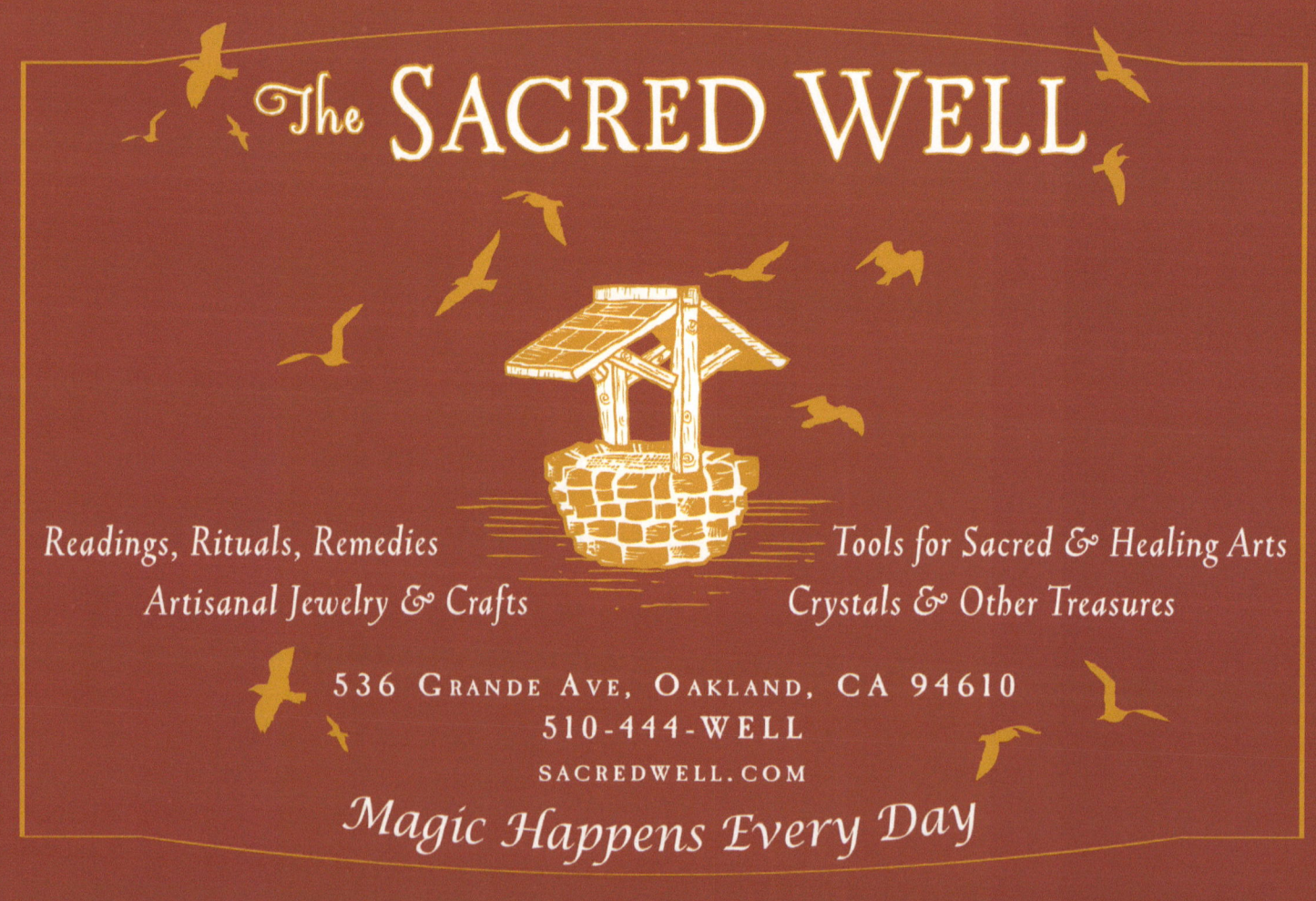

The SACRED WELL

Readings, Rituals, Remedies
Artisanal Jewelry & Crafts

Tools for Sacred & Healing Arts
Crystals & Other Treasures

536 GRANDE AVE, OAKLAND, CA 94610
510-444-WELL
SACREDWELL.COM

Magic Happens Every Day

to wave the heat toward you, naturally because careful to not catch fire from the flame. Visualize that as you're doing this you're actually drawing the fire toward you and over you.

Visualize yourself being washed with the fire and cleansed with the fire. Repeat this process for each of the pieces of paper that you have.

If you choose not to use slips of parchment, you can do this with dried sage leaves. Rather than writing your intentions you'll simply breathe and speak them. Breathe into one side with the intentions of what you wish to release and then breathe into the other side with what you wish to receive. Then drop the leaves into your fire.

After you have finished these steps you'll want to stay with the fire as it burns down. During this time, send prayers to the Gods, commune with your guides, and scry in the flames looking for messages or guidance to show both that your prayer has been received and how to move forward with achieving your goals. The healing is already happening as the fire works to transform your needs, but we still need to do the work. Guidance that you gain from this time can be helpful for once your rite is done and you return to the world of man.

When the fire goes out leave a small offering for the Gods and the fire and say thanks. Then release your guides and ancestors, then the elements, and disperse your circle if you cast one. You can reuse the same cauldron of salts over and over, so there is no need to dump and refill after each use. If it begins to create a hardened surface you can simply break it up with a knife and stir the salts around.

The fire is the most transformative element and it's the swiftest in helping us heal and deal with difficult emotions. Use this ritual any time you need to let go of an emotion or other attachment, including illness. It can also be a helpful part of daily devotional work if you tend to find you deal with a high amount of stress regularly.

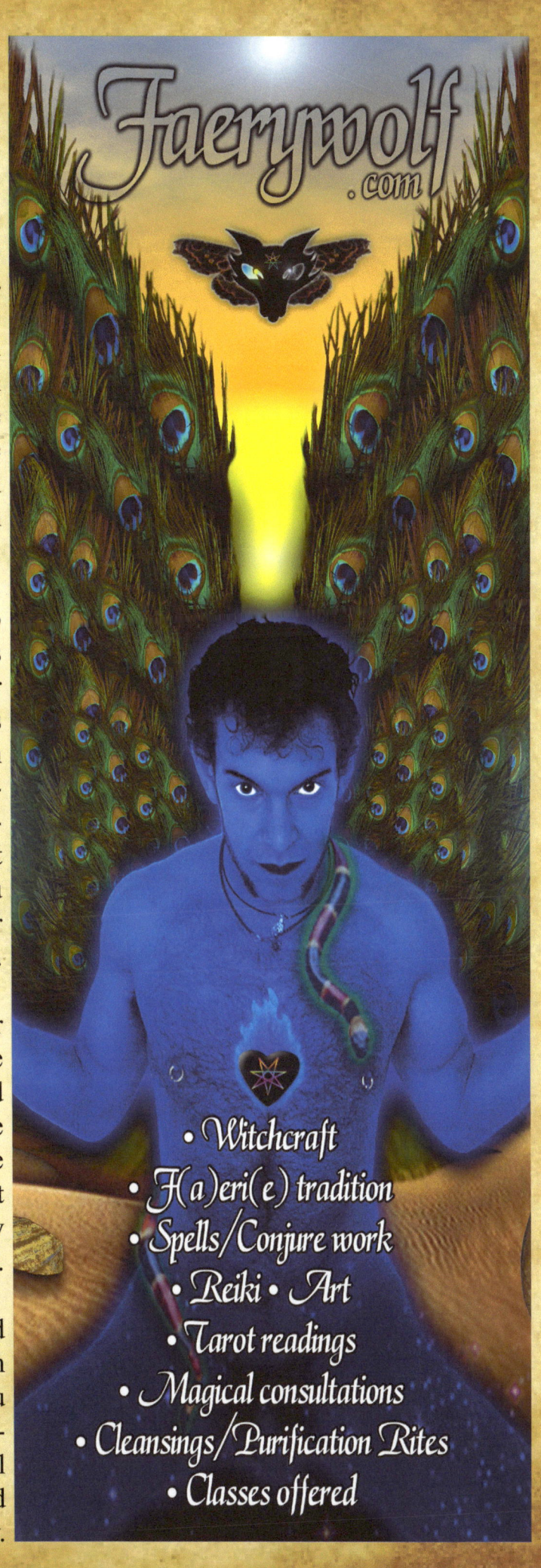

Faerywolf.com

- Witchcraft
- F(a)eri(e) tradition
- Spells/Conjure work
- Reiki • Art
- Tarot readings
- Magical consultations
- Cleansings/Purification Rites
- Classes offered

Being the Now Not the Then

A Witch's Awakening & the Search for Self

By Devin Hunter

The world of witchcraft is a beautiful tapestry woven with the threads of time, these silken threads create a glimmering portrait that is full of divine wisdom and mystical influence. As witches we spin these threads, we create our will into manifestation, however not all of these threads are as sturdy as we would hope. Almost all of the people I come across are those who are seeking answers, transitioning from one stage in life to the next, or in most cases so confused as to what is really the right way to lead a spiritual life. The truth is there is no "right way." It would be easy for me to tell you that being a witch is the one and only way to live your life, and that all other belief systems are overwhelming misguided, however, if I were to say that than I would be lying. Although you already know these truths it is important to look at them once more so you can strengthen each magical thread as you spin it into being for these truths are the raw material that magic is made of.

First, there is no right or wrong way to live your life. We are all given free will from birth, and it is up to us to decide how we use it. In saying that, I have also learned that Karma and Dharma can be a bitch. Life is a constant game of give and take, and no matter what you have done, the good has to balance the bad, the light has to balance the dark, and the day has to balance the night. This idea is the simplest of all our training, but it is sometimes the most forgotten.

Second, we have to love ourselves in order to discover our potential. You have taken the step to advance as a spiritual person, become even more aware of the possibilities that exist in magic, and you have decided to hone in on some skills that you already know exist, let's face it, we don't find magic, it finds us.

So there you are, a person with views that contradict most of society, and that either confuses you, or it pumps you up. You're different, we don't think like most others, we usually don't close our minds to different things that are going on around us, and at the end of the day there is a secret that exists in all of us. Why should we be afraid of that? Why should we fear who we are? If the universe opened up, and gave you a gift that in its purest state was an amazing thing, why run from it? Some of us are lucky enough to have the metaphysical information coursing through our veins from birth, some of us were different thinkers and picked up a book, and some of us wont figure things out until we are much older. To all of the fore-mentioned, Congratulations!

The most amazing thing about the modern craft is that it allows us to be who we want to be, be who we feel we are; it embraces all of its followers. This in some ways is the great thing about not being a part of an organized religion. We don't have a pope telling us what is right or wrong, we don't have a minister telling us that if we don't do exactly what they say we are going to hell, and we certainly only answer to our own moral compass. Because of that we are allowed to be who we are: gay, straight, whatever, it's ok! We can dress the way we choose, we can eat what we like, and no one can tell us we are wrong!

If pagan spirituality can embrace its followers than why can't its followers embrace themselves? It doesn't make too much sense now does it? If we could just take that step to love ourselves a little bit more each day, we could take away the self imposed insecurities and doubts, then free us up to grow as people. As a witch, there is no place for doubt. There is no place for not believing in you. And how are you going to believe in yourself if you don't know your own potential? On that note-how is any one going to believe in you, if you don't believe in yourself?

So, you're a little heavier than other people, a little skinnier than other people, perhaps you have a million freckles on your face? Beautiful! Awesome! You need to pick your battles wisely, and picking one with yourself is not all that wise. We are all made to be just simply who we are. Ask yourself this question, how many doors will open up to you spiritually when you have learned to accept yourself and your potential? I can tell you one thing; the universe isn't going to do it for you.

The hardest thing to do sometimes is to accept your past, your present, and the future. I know it sounds crazy, but these are three very important aspects to our human life. I know people who have spent years trying to get over things that have happened in their past. Can the past haunt you? Yes, but only if you let it. When we talk about dedication the whole idea not only applies to a God or Goddess, but to you as well. We are the present because we were the past.

One philosophy I have adopted is that in life there are victims and non-victims. Victims allow themselves to spend an amazing amount of life force thinking and stressing over the past. They pour their energy into identifying who slighted them, what they didn't do to secure a better future, the negative things about their lives. This can often manifest as depression and anxiety, causing damage not only to themselves but to their future. A non-victim spends their life force on productive means, allowing the past to be the past and the present to be all that is can be. The non-victim chooses to look at the despair of the past and turn it into fuel for their future.

In the present we are constantly being bombarded by everything going on in the world. Most of us enjoy having so many things going on at once, even though we would never admit it, because frankly if you don't have time to introspect, than you don't have to deal with yourself. So where does that leave you? You have the job, the career, the family, but not the self. A lot of us in hitting adulthood forget all about ourselves. Have you ever had that moment where you look in a mirror and can't recognize the person starring back? That happens because you lost touch with yourself, with who you are now. If you don't know who you are now, than how are you going to be that someone you want to be? We are the future, because of the preparations we make in the now.

The future is a bright, beautiful thing. It is all about potential and ability. You can be whatever it is you want to be simply by understanding that you were who you are, and making a plan to secure what you want to be. You want to be a better witch? Than look at your experiences from the past, see where you are now on your path, see your future, and then make plans for it!

We have this ability as magical people to have a connection with the universe that is rarely seen. The key to being an effective witch is solely based on the understanding of yourself, how you affect the universe, and vice-verse. You have to know yourself, you have to trust yourself, and you have to believe in yourself even when no one else will.

You may be asking yourself what all of this has to do with witchcraft; It is all about life-force, how much you have and your relationship to it. A strong witch respects their connection to the universe and respects themselves enough to funnel their life-force into strengthening their being. We can not do the work if we don't have the energy to do it!

A Rite of Self Awareness

A Rite of Self Awareness

To aide yourself as you travel the wonderful path of a modern witch, take a few minutes every day for a week, preferably starting seven days before the full moon, to journal about the hopes and dreams you once had as a child, the hopes and dreams you still have to this day, and the new hopes and dreams that you have acquired in your current life. After journaling finish off this start to your magical transformation by closing your eyes, taking three deep breaths, relaxing your body and repeating, "I am the child of those who came before me, of the ancestors in my blood and the ancestors of my soul. I am love, I am acceptance, I am success, I am the future, and so be it!" On the seventh and final night find a special place that brings you comfort, this may be anything from your altar to your bath tub, light thirteen candles and place them all around you. Close your eyes, as you have before, and take three deep breaths, relaxing your body and mind, then call out to the spirits, "Spirits of love join me this night, Spirits of acceptance join me here! Spirits of success aide me during this rite!" Take a few more slow, steady, deep breaths and once you feel ready to move on with the rite, open your journal from the past week and begin to read aloud your entries by candle light. Once you have finished reading aloud all the past entries spend a few moments contemplating them, visualizing your hopes and dreams becoming reality, and then look up towards the sky and repeat: "I am the child of those who came before me, of the ancestors in my blood and the ancestors of my soul. I am love, I am acceptance, I am success, and I am the future. For all that I was, I am now, for all that I will be, and I am now. My hopes and dreams become my reality, and so shall it become!"

When teaching witches who have been around for a while, as well as new witches I always tell them to keep a journal for this specific purpose. This journal over time has become one of the most powerful and magical items I own. It is full of hopes and prayers, messages to the Gods, and testimonials of magical success. In a way this is a book of shadows. Only the spells that I consider to be my favorite or those spells and rituals that I felt an exceptional connection to the powers that be are written along with the entries in this journal. Only I have access to this journal for it truly has become a book that was written for my eyes and the eyes of the Gods.

Elemental Incense Recipes

Earth

1 part Cedar
1 part Sage
1 part Pine needle
1 part Mandrake

Element of earth and all your trade,
Divine connection shall be made.
Grounded center, solid round,
In you solitude will be found.
Strong and mighty, simple still,
I invoke thee now by witches will!

Air

1 part Eucalyptus
2 parts Lavender
1 part Mugwart

Element of air speed me fast,
Divine connection as I cast.
Quick in task air go round,
Through you messages will be found.
Strong as gale and soft as gust,
I invoke thee now in you I trust!

Spirit

1 part Frankincense
1 part Mugwart
1 part Sage
1 part Cedar

Element Akasha and spirit fare,
Divine connection with you I pair.
Ancestral energies found in me,
The third in which I see.
Strong as Gods, simple as all,
I invoke thee now, spirit I call!

Fire

1 part Tobacco
1 part Cinnamon
1 part Clove
1 part Vanilla bean

Element of fire you I sire,
Divine connection I desire.
Destruction, Creation, Embers burn,
By your passion I will learn.
Strong as sun, simple as spark,
I invoke thee now to light the dark!

Water

1 part Willow bark
1 part Heather
1 part Star anise
1 part Rose petals

Element of water flow through me,
Divine connection set me free.
Purity, Love, and Unconscious mind,
Through your strength influence I'll find.
Strong as Tsunami, gentle as tide,
I invoke thee now to be my guide!

She hummed the song it was as the buzzing of bees (or a top spinning round), a spinning-wheel spinning life.

She spun the lives of all men; all things were spun from the wheel of Diana. Lucifer turned the wheel.

And having made the heavens and the stars and the rain, Diana became Queen of the Witches; she was the cat who ruled the star-mice, the heaven and the rain.

-Aradia: Gospel of the witches- Leland
1897

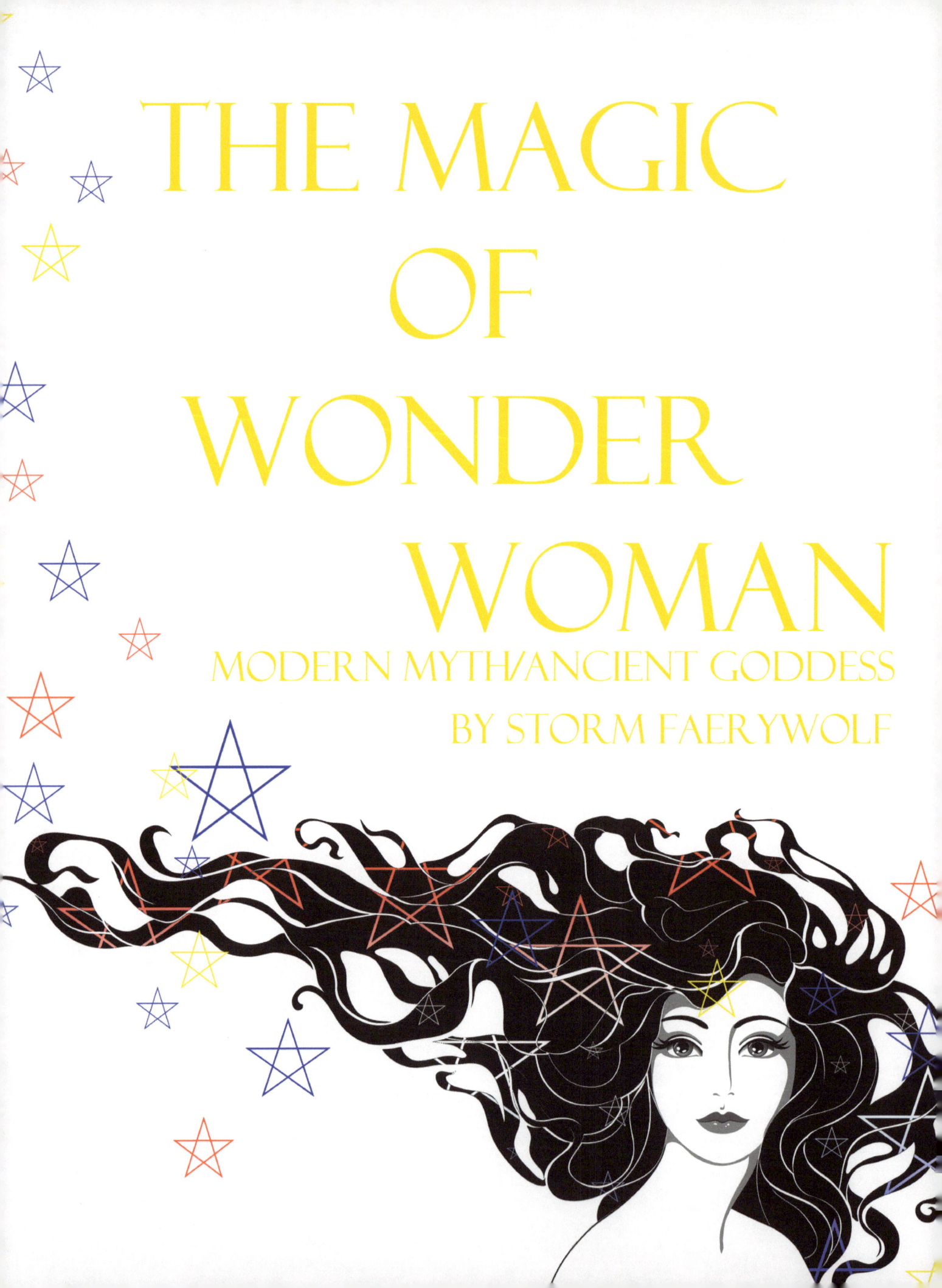

Let me begin this missive by stating that it is my sincere belief that the character "Wonder Woman", the beloved super-heroine of comic book fame, is a modern form of an ancient Goddess. Though some might scoff at such an assertion, I mean it with all the sincerity and deep spiritual reverence that a person of considerable devotion can offer.

My faith in this claim is based on personal experience, but also in hearing the stories of others who have shared similar views. When I previously wrote about Wonder Woman as a spiritual and magical focal pointi, I was not prepared for the amount of correspondence I would receive from those who felt the same. A common theme began to emerge that painted a picture of those who saw in this beloved character a shining ray of hope and even evolution. Her stories made people think; about right and wrong, about culture and devotion, about violence and peace. She inspired people to live better lives, to hold true to their highest ideals, even when the situation seemed bleak.

It is taught in some traditional witchcraft circles that the works of certain artists, writers, and poets carry within them glimpses of the Otherworld; messages from the hidden power of the land, the spirits, the faeries, or the Godsii. Certain authors, such as J.R.R. Tolkien and H.P. Lovecraft, have been regarded as oracles of this hidden kingdom, describing in their fictional tales and histories spiritual truths that can assist us in our quest for knowledge of the numinous. Once we accept that some artists and authors may be "tuned in" to the powers-that-be, it is not so much of a leap to then realize that this might extend to all artistic genres, even the popular comic book.

Wonder Woman was created with the Goddess in mind. She was named after the Goddess Diana whom the ancient Romans had known as a virgin moon goddess, a goddess of the hunt, and of childbirth and whose origins stretch back into ancient Italy, where she was regarded as the Queen of the Witches.

"If the prospect of living in a world where trying to respect the basic rights of those around you--and valuing each other simply because we exist--are such daunting, impossible tasks that only a super-hero born of royalty can address them...then what sort of world are we left with? And what sort of world do you want to live in?"
-Diana, *Wonder Woman #170*, by Jimenez & Kelly

The fictional character first appeared in 1941 in All Star Comics #8 and was created by Charles Moulton (the pen name of William Moulton Marston) a psychologist and inventor of the lie detector. Moulton was a feminist theorist and was driven by the idea that young women needed powerful role models. In 1943 he wrote for The American Scholar magazine on the subject: "Not even girls want to be girls so long as our feminine archetype lacks force, strength, and power. Not wanting to be girls, they don't want to be tender, submissive, peace-loving as good women are. Women's strong qualities have become despised because of their weakness. The obvious remedy is to create a feminine character with all the strength of Superman plus all the allure of a good and beautiful woman."

Consistently Wonder Woman has stood as an example of strength for women and girls wanting to make it in "man's world". Especially in the era of her creation women were explicitly taught to remain quiet and to put their own needs and desires aside so that they could attend to the needs and desires of the men in their lives. In the face of this gender-based oppression Wonder Woman stood tall to show women of all ages that there is another way.

In standing up for women's equality, Wonder Woman also inspired another group of people: gay men. By embodying the qualities of peace, love, compassion, and truth –alongside those of strength, skill, intelligence, and cunning –Wonder Woman showed the world that there are alternatives to the much publicized version of strength as embodied by the culture of men;

that of arrogance, aggression, and dominance. Those stereotypically "masculine" qualities that I intuitively rejected as a young queer boy in the 1970's, identifying instead with those espoused by strong female role models whose characters resonated with my own soul. Wonder Woman didn't just want to "beat up the bad guy" (no matter how good she might look doing it!); she wanted to win hearts, minds, and souls... she wanted to educate and elevate the level of discourse to promote the "Amazonian ideals" of peace, love, strength, and freedom. More often than not, she wanted to reason with the evil-doer, often persuading them to reform.

Those who have followed her various incarnations from comic book, to cartoon, to television series, and more, have seen in her stories the stuff that myths are made from. True myths are the stories that speak to our souls. They reach inside us and elevate us so that we can get a better look at God; and in doing so, ourselves. This is what sets them apart from a "mere" work of fiction. They inspire us to really look at what we value by tapping into what we feel. These stories and the symbols depicted within them are avenues by which we are able to grasp a deeper understanding of ourselves in relation to the universe, through principal players within the myth. Whether they reflect actual events or are comprised entirely of wholesale fabrication (it matters not which) they communicate via the realm of symbolic to our deep sub-consciousness. In short, myths invite us to better ourselves.

For those not familiar with the iconic story of Wonder Woman I will attempt to relay it here, knowing full well that –like so many deeper spiritual teachings—her story is a mystery that cannot be fully told, only experienced. This is because her tale is not static, but bardic; key points changing with every retelling that serve to expand the depth of meaning for the tale, rather than to detract from it. Over the years her origin story has been retold, again and again; adding an element here, re-visioning an event or a relationship there... and sometimes completely contradicting itself and even restarting completely. In this we see the same patterns as in the ancient myths, with family trees being rewritten, origin myths being retold with different attributes... even human beings being elevated to godhood... and the story of Wonder Woman is no different.

Her original myth places her on "Paradise Island", later called 'Themyscira'; an island inhabited by a tribe of women, the Amazons of myth. They were the reincarnated souls of women who had been killed by men throughout history, granted immortality by the ancient gods to live in seclusion, free from the contaminating influence of men. In this woman's paradise the Amazons formed a utopian society and excelled in science, art, athletics, and mathematics.

As the story goes, Hippolyta, Queen of the Amazons, desired a child above all else. Being without a way to have one of her own, she formed a baby out of clay and prayed to the Gods to give the image life. The Godsi appeared and answered her prayers, blessing the child princess with attributes of their heavenly power. Named, Diana after the Goddess of the Hunt and the Moon, she excelled in all of the Amazonian arts, performed amazing feats of strength and skill, and eventually grew into a formidable warrior and scholar.

In the original story she falls in love with Steve Trevor, an American fighter pilot who crash landed on the mythical island after being shot down by Nazi forces during World War II. Having decided that the Nazis present a definite danger to the world, Queen Hippolyta announces a contest to determine which of her Amazons will accompany Trevor back to "Man's World" and act in defense of democracy. Diana is forbidden to enter the contest, but does so anyway wearing a mask to conceal her identity. Diana easily defeats all of her opponents and earns the right to become the ambassador to the outside world dressed in the colors and symbols of the American flag to show her allegiance.

In another version the Amazons have been charged with defending the world from an ancient evil that is imprisoned beneath their island. In this version a female pilot, Diana Trevor, crash lands on their island and is instrumental in saving the lives of Amazons when that evil is accidentally released from its prison. Trevor sacrifices herself in order to save others, an act that earns her deep respect among the Amazons. In death, the Amazons honor her as one of their own, creating formal garb from her military uniform and a tattered American flag, forming the basis for the iconic armor that Wonder Woman possesses. The contest is then enacted to determine who will be the ambassador to "Patriarch's World", and Diana wins this honor.

In her various tales she has lost and regained her powers several times, lost and regained (and lost again) her immortality, lived as a human among us, and was even elevated to Godhood among the Olympian deities as Diana, Goddess of Truth… only to return to earth as an avatar of the Olympian deities once more. In a more recent retelling, her origins from clay are said to have been a cover for her true origins as a daughter of Zeus.

As with most ancient Gods she is in possession of magical artifacts. While all Amazons wear silver slave bracelets as reminders of when they were enslaved at the hands of men, Diana's silver bracelets are formed from the aegis of Athena and are capable of deflecting any weapon. Her unbreakable golden lasso was formed from the golden girdle of Gaea and burns with the fires of Hestia; compelling those who are bound with it to speak only the truth. Her golden tiara, symbol of the monarchy, is a magical throwing weapon… she even had an invisible plane that responds to her mental commands (or, occasionally, an invisible Pegasus-drawn chariot) variously depicted as being of Amazonian technology, the mythical Pegasus transformed, an invention of Batman's given to her as a gift, or even a telepathic shape-shifting alien being.

Over the years, and the many retellings of her story, certain patterns have emerged that seem to form the "mythical core" of Wonder Woman as an actual Goddess. She is consistently depicted as fighting for freedom and truth; engaging the world in a way that is selfless and aligned toward the good of all life. One of the most inspiring of her stories, in my opinion, comes from the pages of a 2001 graphic novel and involves her wrapping her magic lasso of truth around herself in order to become aware and purified of any potential self-deception that might lead to her misusing her power: "She's seen what unchecked power can do, even to those with the best of intentions. Her single GREATEST fear, the thing that harries her across her dreams—is that SHE will one day TURN from the path of truth, and become a DESTROYER."[i]

Her stories have inspired people to claim their own power and to live meaningful lives in the face of adversity. To me this alone begins to reveal her power as a modern face of the Goddess. But to really feel her power, we should do what any good witch or warlock would do and that's to invoke her.

INVOKING WONDER WOMAN

As is my preference for working with any deity, I advise building an altar to her. Adorn it with images of her to your liking. There are a plethora of them to be found on the internet, or you could purchase one of the many collectible statues that are available.

Get five candles, red, white, blue, silver, and gold; her sacred colors. Place them in a pentacle around whatever central image you have. Do any grounding/centering/aligning exercises that you are accustomed to, including Casting a Circle, if desired. (Using a golden cord as a circle for this rite is especially potent, as you can imagine.) An optional addition to this rite would be to play some music that you feel is appropriate to the working; I personally have worked with version of the Wonder Woman theme song from the 1970's television show.

Shop online for our great selection of spiritual supplies

Herbs   Oils   Incense   Soaps   Candles   & More

www.TheMysticDream.com

We offer many spiritual services such as...

Setting Lights   Reiki   Custom Mojos
Tarot   Spells & Altar Work   Classes

Where Ancient Wisdom Meets the New Aeon

1437 N Broadway
Walnut Creek, CA 94596
925-933-2342
Open 7 Days

Light the candles one at a time in turn while saying:
(RED) "I invoke Diana; strength of the warrior."
(WHITE) "I invoke Diana; ambassador of peace."
(BLUE) "I invoke Diana; compassion and love!"
(SILVER) "I invoke Diana; shield and protect."
(GOLD) "I invoke Diana; shining light of truth."

Focus your attention on your central image. With an open heart, reach out to her presence. Pray over all the candles at once and imagine their light shining toward the center, combining together to empower your central image. Say:

"Formed from clay of Paradise
and brought to life by Goddess power
You are the champion of your sisters
You left your home to teach men peace."

Allow your awareness to be softly open; just notice how you feel in this space for her that you have created.

Here now you may make any specific prayers or petitions you wish. Depending on your situation you may wish to focus more heavily on one or more of her aspects (warrior, peacemaker, lover, protector, truth seeker, etc.) Speak aloud a heartfelt prayer, asking her to guide you… to give you strength, protection, etc. Take your time.

When you are finished, thank her with a prayer of your own making. Extinguish the candles in reverse order. If you used a golden cord you may wish to tie this around your waist in order to "seal" the power of the rite within you. Just don't try to tell any lies while you are wearing it!

Whether you connect to this image as a modern form of the Goddess, or as simply an egregore or magical thought-form, the image and mythos of Wonder Woman can be a potent tool in our magic to inspire us to strive toward our highest ideals in the presence of difficulty. With her image and stories touching so many people over so many years, the current of energy is quite strong, just waiting for the magically minded to "tap into" it, so as to feed our magic. May her beauty and wisdom guide us all.
For the Glory of Gaea!

EARTH WARRIORS FESTIVAL
BATTLE CRY 2012

WWW.EARTHWARRIORSFESTIVAL.COM

THE PREMIERE FESTIVAL FOR THOSE WHO WALK THE WARRIOR AND GUARDIAN PATHS. EARTH WARRIORS IS A 21+ EVENT IN THE HEART OF OHIO AND HAS BEEN FEATURED ON THE MODERN WITCH PODCAST. CABINS, MEAL PLANS, WARRIOR GAMES, AND WORKSHOPS BY TODAY'S LEADING PAGAN AUTHORS, MUSICIANS, AND MORE!

Burning Windows
Ceromancy With Glass Encased Candles
By Chas Bogan

Your magic talks back to you. Every action that takes place amidst your spell work serves as an omen. This is evidenced most clearly with candle magic. The manner in which your candle burns indicates how your desires will manifest. It may tell you that things will take a long time, or be fraught with obstacles; or it may tell you that what you wish for is not ultimately in your best interest. The messages given in ceromancy (the divination of candles) speak differently depending on what type of candle is being burned. This article will examine ceromancy with glass encased candles, alternatively known as 'seven day candles' and 'devotional candles.'

A quick note about these candles… Originally poured with the purpose of lasting seven days, the materials used in these candles have weakened over time, so that these days such a candle may burn for only five days depending on its quality. My local supermarket sells these candles in their Mexican food section, and they are crap, skinny little things that last only a few days and never seem to burn all the way down. For magic they are unacceptable. Although a good magician is able to use whatever is on hand, finding quality magical tools and ingredients is important. Half-assed materials lead to half-assed results. Especially if you are expecting to read the messages left on a devotional candle then you will need one of quality. It is worth the trip to your local spiritual supply store or an online retailer of quality. An appropriate candle in my opinion should be approximately 8 inches high and just under 3 inches wide. The wax should be soft enough that you can push a screwdriver into it with minimal effort.

Before I discuss how to read the burn let me briefly describe how to dress a devotional candle. First you may want to cleanse it, which can easily be done by wiping it with a washcloth, perhaps one that has been wetted with a spiritual cleaner such as Florida Water. Next, you may choose to dress it with oil; there are many conjure oils on the market that are aligned with specific needs. After choosing one that is right for your work you may simply pour a small amount on top of the wax (not too much or it will drown the wick), however a more thorough way is to take something long and firm, such as a screwdriver or dowel, and poke holes down into the wax (I tend to make three holes), then pour some of the oil into the holes. After that you can add some glitter of an appropriate color, and/or herbs aligned with your goal. We will see that this glitter and herbal residue may stick to the glass in a manner insightful for ceromancy. Having done all that you will want to tell the candle what its purpose is, and for this you will need to draw on the glass, which I find is done most easily with a Sharpie. How you do this is up to you. You can draw a picture or write out the things you want in words, however I do like for there to be a definite front and back to the candle for reasons I will do into later.

Alright, so let's say you have done all that. There is of course much more that you could do, such as creating a petition paper or reciting a specific psalm or chant, but I will leave that to your discretion. The manner in which you light your candle is likewise your business; however I will encourage you to spend a bit of time bonding with it. In lighting this candle you are creating a living spirit. Take some time to gaze at it. Acknowledge its life. See the aura of light surrounding it. Here is the soul of your spell, the spirit that will do your magical bidding. You must tell it what you need. Because it was born from you, it speaks your language, so do not fear being plain spoken. Additionally, it will speak back to you in a symbolic language that you understand. What will follow in this article are the ways in which candles speak to me, which is a combination of traditional Conjure Ceromancy and some things that I have picked up from other spiritual workers or my own experiences. Ultimately however the candle will speak to you by means of whatever symbolic language you learn.

First we should discuss the language of the flame itself. The following are meanings attributed to such behavior:

A low flame indicates that the work will take time. Whatever you asked for may not manifest quickly. Depending on what the spell is for you may try to speed things up, such as by pouring a few drops of Fast Luck oil into your wax.

A High flame indicated that things are going quickly. The Universe has heard your plea and change is coming.

A popping flame quite literally means that the candle has something to tell you. The interpretation depends on what the candle is for. Overall, it indicates that there is something that needs you attention, perhaps something that has been overlooked and needs to be sorted out before success can come. It also can indicate that someone may be talking behind your back; you may add some Stop Gossip oil to the wax. If you have lit the candle for protection then beware, things are being said or done behind your back.

A double can indicate different things depending on the purpose of the candle. Examine your feelings to make sure that you are not of two minds about what you are doing. In love magic it can be a positive sign of romantic pairing. If the candle was lit for protective work, then the double flame asserts that you do not stand alone, but have the help of other persons or spiritual powers.

A jumping flame speaks of anger. You may have resentments that must come to the surface and be dealt with before you can move forward and your spell become fully manifest. Or this could be the anger of another, someone who is holding you back. Spend some time gazing into this jumping flame and see what emotions arise in you or what your intuition has to say.

Sparks from a candle, so long as they don't catch anything on fire, are beneficial. It is a display of power from your candle, and so long as the remainder of it burns clean then you should be powerfully blessed.

Sometimes the flame will point in a specific direction, and this can also have meaning. Since I am versed in Western Magical traditions which have certain correspondences given to the various directions I associate the East with knowledge, South with lust, West with emotions, and the North with respite. Therefore if a flame reached east for a noticeable period of time then I would have to ask myself if I had all the knowledge I needed in order to manifest this spell, perhaps that job I am working for has crappy benefits or a boss who'll hate me. A southward reaching flame might tell me that things will be getting spicy, which would be good news for a romance, although for other types of work this could indicate that rivals will be worked up against me. West tells me to be aware of my emotions, as well as those of whomever I may be doing work for. Finally, North tells me to slow down, and that my ability to control destiny might best be enhanced by grounding myself and letting go. Additionally a directional flame may be pointing you in a specific direction, such as if you are doing work to enable you to move then this flame may be telling you which direction to go.

Before I go on to talk about residue left on the glass I want to address the issue of lighting and relighting candles. If you are unable to leave your candle burning continuously be aware that each time you snuff it out and relight it you are likely to cause lines of wax to collect. Which brings us to our first category of wax reading…

Lines of wax (Horizontal): These often indicate obstacles, challenges that will need to be met in the process of attaining whatever your candle was lit for.

Lines of wax (Vertical): For me these indicate being trapped. When seen on a court case candle they can also indicate that jail time will be an issue.

There are two things to take note of regarding the wax. When I mentioned earlier that I like there to be a definite front and back to a candle it is because the position of wax residue speaks to the situation. Therefore lines of wax in the back remark about what is behind you, whereas lines in front indicate what lies ahead. Also, if you have added glitter or herbs to your candle they may also adhere to the lines of wax. When I see these it tells me that these obstacles, difficult as they may be, will ultimately be to my benefit, and that positive lessons will be learned from them.

Of course there are many shapes that the wax may take. If you see something distinctive, such as the shape of a key, then you may divine its meaning in the same manner as you would were a key to appear in your dream. A good book on dream symbols may be helpful if you do not have an immediate understanding of what a certain symbol means for you.

In addition to what the wax tells you, the soot also indicates the conditions surrounding your magic. A sooty candle may or may not be a bad thing, in that the blackness represents the negativity your candle has burned through to achieve your goal. Nonetheless, when a candle of mine burns sooty I start over, reexamining the situation and my approach, doing an uncrossing or other form of cleaning work to further remove any negative energy, then burn another candle which hopefully will burn cleaner and suggest that my magical work has progressed.

There are other signs that the energy you have sent out with your candle has encountered trouble. If you candle cracks, if it fails to burn down all the way, or gods forbid it catches something around it on fire, then there is a lot more work you need to do. This indicates that you are in a spiritual battle. The enemy may be another person who is doing work against you, or the enemy may be yourself if you are not wholeheartedly certain that what you are doing is best or ethical.

Once your candle has finished it is important to properly dispose of it. I do this with Florida Water, pouring some inside and swirling it around. You may wish to wet a rag with it and remove whatever symbols you have draw on your candle. Your candle has done its magic, and therefore the glass is like the cocoon left behind by the butterfly. For ecological reasons I put mine in the recycling after it has been properly cleansed.

Contibutor Bios

David Salisbury
David Salisbury is a queer, vegan, Witch and Pagan organizer in Washington, DC. A Wiccan priest with The Firefly House, David works with several other organizations including The Open Hearth Foundation, Pagan Newswire Collective, and Pagan Pride Day.

Tim Titus
Tim is a high school teacher who moonlights as a journalist for all things witchy. He is a regular contributor to The Juggler, a Pagan Newswire Collective blog on culture and pop culture, and the Temple Bell, newsletter for the Temple of Witchcraft. He is also one of the co-founders of the Pagan Newswire Collective's Southern California Bureau, reporting on Pagan news from the Orange County/LA area.

Elayne Lockhart
Elayne Lockhart is a 4th generation witch living in Northern California. She teaches and lectures in the local pagan community. Elayne currently serves on the Board of Directors for The Order of the Sacred Wheel. elaynelockhart@yahoo.com www.elaynelockhart.blogspot.com

Gede Parma
Gede Parma is a Witch, Pagan Mystic, initiated Priest and award-winning author. He is an initiate and teacher of the WildWood Tradition of Witchcraft, a hereditary healer and seer with Balinese-Celtic ancestry and an enthusiastic writer. Gede is a proactive and dynamic teacher and is also the creator and facilitator of the two-year Shamanic Craft Apprenticeship. He teaches the Craft, Magick and Pagan Mysteries internationally. You can visit Gede at www.gedeparma.com

Taylor Ellwood
Taylor Ellwood is the author of the forthcoming book Magical Identity, as well as Pop Culture Magick, Space/Time Magic and a few other occult books. He's also the managing Non-Fiction Editor of Immanion Press. For more information about his latest project and classes, please visit http://www.magicalexperiments.com

Heather Killen

Heather is a third degree high priestess in Gardnerian Wicca, a full time mom, shop owner, and the organizaer for the Earth Warriors Festival. When she is not blending spa quality bath and body products, raising two young boys, and teaching Heather can be found as an active pagan community member. For more information visit her at www.VioletFlameGifts.com

Storm Faerywolf

Storm Faerywolf is an artist, writer, poet, teacher, and initiate of the F(a)eri(e) tradition of witchcraft. He has been practicing the Craft for over 25 years and teaching for more than 15. He has lead open circles, given lectures, and taught public and private classes in the San Francisco Bay Area and across the U.S. He holds the Black Wand of sorcery and is the founder of his own line of Feri, BlueRose. He is the author of The Stars Within the Earth, and the editor of WitchEye: A Journal of Feri Uprising. For more information about his classes or his art visit his website at www.faerywolf.com.

Chas Bogan

I am an artist and mystic, having studied and practiced many diverse forms of metaphysics for the past 25 years. That experience is reflected in my art, which ranges from the design of unique divination tools to various other forms of sacred expression. My shamanic talents have lead me to create various collections of spiritual supplies crafted for Modern Conjure Brand, such as baths, oils, powders, waters; and more. I am available for consultations and spiritual work by appointment Fridays, Saturdays and Sundays; during which I may be serving my clients in my capacity as a Reiki Master Teacher; Rootworker; Tarot Reader; Conjure Doctor; and teacher of various magical arts including the Feri Tradition of which I am an initiate.

Yeshe Rabbit

Yeshe Rabbit is a lifelong witch, Presiding High Priestess of Come As You Are Coven (www.cayacoven.org), co-owner and tarot reader at The Sacred Well (www.sacredwell.com), and a devotee of the Great Mother Goddess. Read more of her musings at www.wayoftherabbit.com

Devin Hunter

Devin is the host of the Modern Witch Podcast and Design editor for Modern Witch Magazine. Devin is an internationally recognized metaphysical and spiritual teacher and has been featured in publications such as Moon Shadows Magazine. Currently Devin is the House Medium and store manager for The Mystic Dream in Walnut Creek California. Devin leads The Living Temple of Diana as Head Priest and tours both nationally and internationally.

Rowan Pendragon

Rowan Pendragon is a Priestess, blogger, author, and a tarot professional currently living just outside of Salem, MA. She has been a Witch for over 25 years and has been working professionally with the public for over 10 years. Rowan is a Certified Tarot Consultant, Certified Paranormal Investigator, Certified Angel Communication Master, Usui Reiki Master Teacher, Faery Reiki Master, and a Registered Metaphysical Practitioner with the World Metaphysical Association. She has studied Wicca, Witchcraft, and Paganism with some fantastic teachers including Janet Farrar and Gavin Bone, Christopher Penczak, and Raven and Stephanie Grimassi.

Notes

www.ingramcontent.com/pod-product-compliance
Lightning Source LLC
Chambersburg PA
CBHW042000150426
43194CB00002B/76